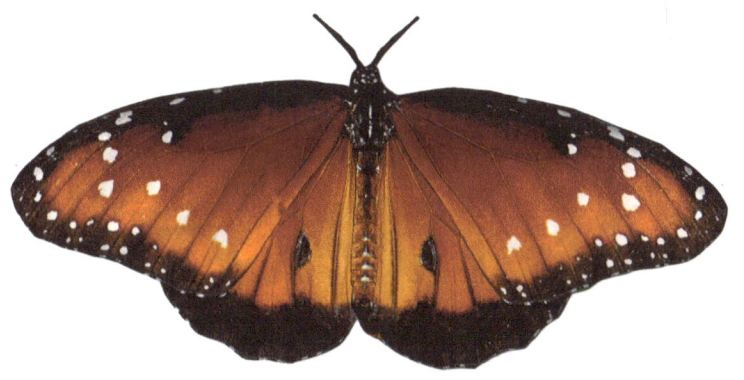

Butterfly at Daybreak

The Complete Guidebook for Self-Discovery and Enjoyment

—using basic collage

Ginny McIntosh, LISW and Gale C. Vance, LCSW

Butterfly At Daybreak

The Complete Guidebook for Self-Discovery and Enjoyment
—using basic collage

©2007 Ginny McIntosh, LISW And Gale C. Vance, LCSW

Published by 1st World Publishing
1100 North 4th St. Suite 131, Fairfield, Iowa 52556
tel: 641-209-5000 • fax: 641-209-3001
web: www.1stworldpublishing.com

First Edition

LCCN: 2006938769

SoftCover ISBN: 1-4218-9902-7

This material has been written and published solely for educational purposes. The authors and the publisher shall have neither liability nor responsibility to any person or entity with respect to any loss, damage or injury caused or alleged to be caused directly or indirectly by the information contained in this book.

In some cases, to protect confidentiality, we have used pseudonyms for the collage makers.

Book design by Liz Howard. liz@lizhowardgraphics@yahoo.com

Cover image, "Butterfly At Daybreak" is taken from the collage on page 85.

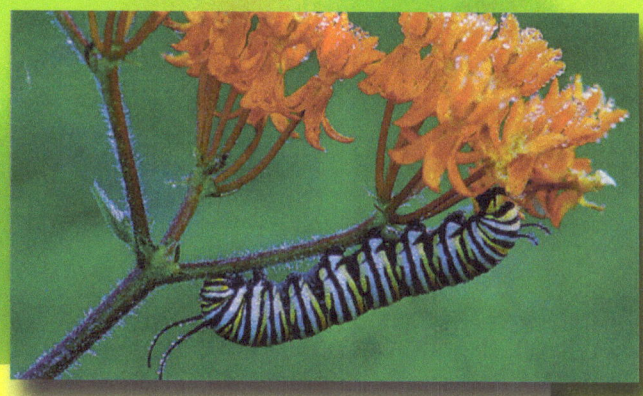

We dedicate this book to the amazing caterpillar.

The Biological Story Of Butterfly Metamorphosis

The striped caterpillar you have just encountered on your morning walk has been energetically eating many times its weight each day. Soon it will form a chrysalis and hang quietly. Inside its cocooned body, imaginal discs start to form. At first the caterpillar's immune system is alarmed and destroys the discs. But as time goes on, more and more discs begin to quickly form into clusters, overwhelming the caterpillar's immune system. The caterpillar's body dissolves into a soupy liquid which feeds the discs as they now become full-grown imaginal cells. These cells develop into the body of the butterfly, an extraordinary metamorphosis of one thing into another.

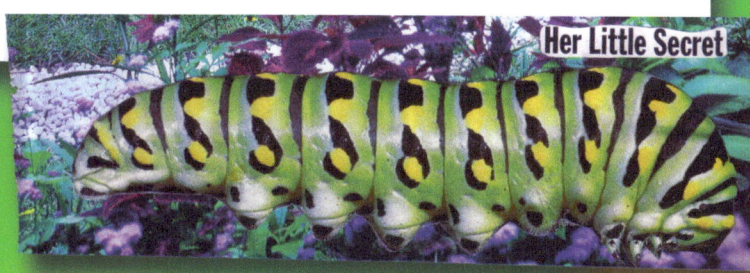

Her Little Secret

ACKNOWLEDGEMENTS

Heartfelt thanks to our friends and family members who have encouraged and supported us through this book-making process and thanks to our friend Nancy Ging who first suggested we write this book. We also wish to thank our students and colleagues who have joined us in making collages and who have freely shared their stories. Thanks to our photographers, especially Michael and Laura Farrell. Chris Carlson helped us get the book typed and created a preliminary design.

Editor and author Barbara Boulden gave us critical feedback which led us to our energetic, upbeat editor Sue Savage who kept our noses to the grindstone as we wrote our second draft. Special thanks to graphic designer Liz Howard who worked with us to present our book in full, inviting color. Thanks to the anonymous artists and photographers whose pictures we cut and pasted to create new images. We would love to credit every one of you and will, in our next printing, if you let us know who you are.

ABOUT THE AUTHORS

Ginny McIntosh

Ginny McIntosh, MSW, LISW, is a Licensed Independent Social Worker and expressive arts therapist, and is also trained as a nurse. Since 1990, she has worked at community mental health agencies with survivors of sexual abuse and domestic violence. She has also worked as a community organizer, training people in community building and leadership skills.

Ginny enjoys providing expressive arts experiences for women's groups, retreats, church groups and college classes. She provides expressive arts education for professional counselors, aiding them in integrating expressive arts techniques into traditional psychotherapy practice.

She and her husband live in Fairfield, Iowa.

Gale Vance

Gale C. Vance, MSW, LCSW, is a clinical social worker in private practice. She has taught courses in couple counseling, relationship building, communication skills and group dynamics at the college level as well as courses in coping with divorce, expressive art and early childhood parental loss.

Gale has led long-term groups for adults molested as children, physically abused spouses, divorce adjustment, couple communication and motherless daughters as well as weekend workshops focusing on personal growth and creativity. She has spent many years training volunteers to handle phone hotlines for women in crisis.

She lives in Downers Grove, Illinois and continues to make time for her art and her family.

The authors can be contacted at
butterfly@lisco.com

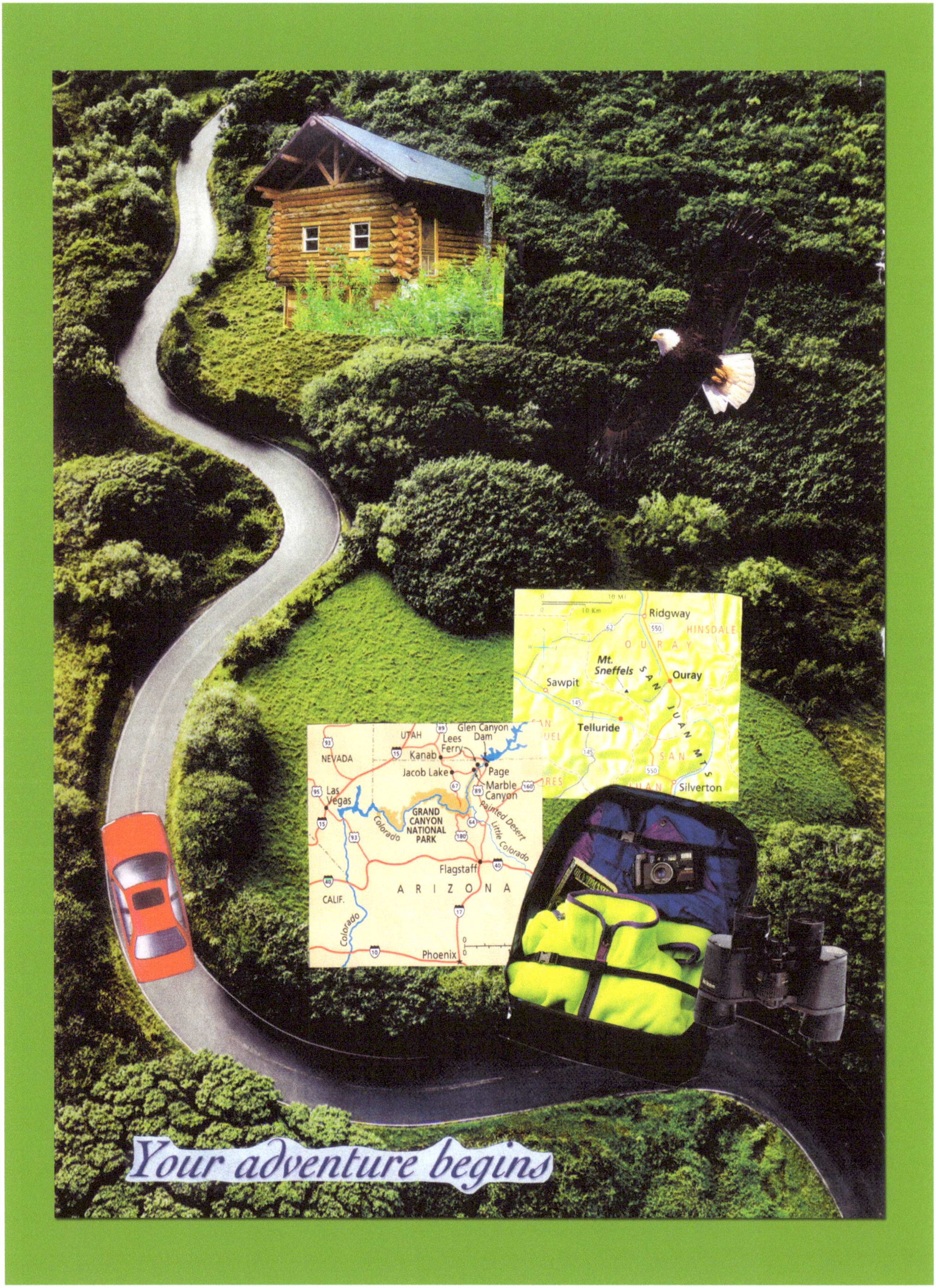

Your adventure begins

TABLE OF CONTENTS

A Road Map For Your Journey

Each person is at a different place on his or her collage making journey depending upon experience. Some may have made several collages, while others may be making their very first one. If you are just beginning you can start with our Welcome section and Chapter 1. If you are an experienced collage maker you may want to read other chapters for new ideas. To help you decide where you want to start, here is a brief synopsis of each chapter.

All the basics are here to get you started on your journey.

Help in expressing strong feelings such as sadness, anger, or anxiety is offered here. If you have a burning question or a current challenge in your life and are looking for insight and direction, read this chapter. You will also find guidance on expressing thoughts and feelings about political, social and environmental issues. And you will learn how collage making can add comfort, playfulness and relaxation to your life. Finally, you will learn how to converse with your collage to hear the voice of your deep inner wisdom.

Exploring memories can be important. This chapter takes you on a journey into your past.

Do you want to journey inside yourself? Using the symbol of the tree, the focus here is to find out more about who you really are and develop a greater appreciation of your complexity and richness.

Everyone faces transitions throughout their lives. Using the symbol of the bridge, we explore transitions in career and relationships as well as retirement and other life-style changes.

Use your favorite fairy tales and childhood songs to explore the transformation from your childhood self to the person you are now.

For access to your imagination and intuition try the guided imagery presented here. Use it as a springboard to a collage making experience.

A Road Map For Your Journey *continued*

Each chapter begins with brief directions followed by examples created by collage makers.

Our advice for your journey is to start simply. Move at a comfortable pace. Try new things. Do things your way. Experience the awe of who you are and where you're headed. We hope you enjoy your journey as much as we are enjoying ours.

—Gale and Ginny

Welcome

Every child is a painter.
The problem is how to remain an artist once he grows up.
—Pablo Picasso

Your "Inner" Artist

We are all naturally creative. The problem is, as Picasso says, how do we remain so when we grow up? Too many of us were told as children that art is supposed to conform to certain acceptable standards. These expectations tend to stifle our inner desire to create. Given its freedom, however, your inner artist will happily surprise you as you begin working on your collages. Colorful, meaningful collages are made every day by people with no formal art training. In fact, in this entire guidebook only two of the collages are from contributors who were trained in the fine arts. All of the other collages were made by people who took the risk of unlocking their inner artist.

What Is A Collage?

Images have the power to capture our reality and dreams. When you combine images, such as simple magazine pictures and/or photos into a collage you increase the power of each individual image. Collage making is the simple process of combining objects and images which already exist into something which never existed. Adriana Diaz in her book, *Freeing the Creative Spirit*, says "Collage is the art of pasting, sewing, or affixing materials to a surface." She adds, "At a time when recycling may be a key to planetary survival, we could say that collage is the perfect art form for the ecological age." You will see a variety of materials used in collages in this book each representing something special to the collage.

Why Making A Collage Is Helpful

Every time you make a collage, you will learn something new about yourself. You will be interested and even amazed by the wisdom that emerges when you simply put your images together and get to know them. In some mysterious way the images will cut through to your deepest core. Once there, you will become better acquainted with the richness of your own inner being.

Collage making will help you express your feelings in a safe manner, sharpen your intuition, explore life themes such as change, gather insights into difficulties, find answers to problems, increase your self-esteem and recover your imagination. Collage can also be used for play and relaxation or to forget more serious matters for a moment. Many of those who use collage in this way say they experience a change in perspective. They see things with new eyes, seeing familiar things differently. In every case, you will learn something about yourself, replenish your energy, and add richness to your life.

Beyond Beauty

For most primal people, including indigenous Americans, beauty was an occasional by-product of the art-making process, not the primary purpose. "The intended outcome of image and art making," according to Peter London, author of *No More Secondhand Art*, "was a search for personal and collective power and well-being…an instrument of communion between the self and all that is important, all that is sacred." Many of your collages may not look beautiful to you. They will, however, illustrate the insights that are true for you now.

Using Your Left And Right Brain

The creative process is a product of the "right" brain, which is the non-verbal, intuitive and imaginative side. In our culture and in school we are taught to think mostly with the "left" brain—the more analytical, verbal, fact-oriented side. Many people now propose that using both sides of the brain creates an integrated, or whole-brain process that produces the most creative solutions to personal and community problems.

Albert Einstein believed that our community and international problems would not be solved at the level of thinking on which they were created. He said, "Imagination is more important than knowledge" in arriving at these solutions. Collage making will stretch your imagination and develop your intuitive skills. You will become more of a whole-brain problem-solver.

Expressive Arts And The Healing Process

Words, when used to talk or to journal can only take you so far. Sometimes when looking for a solution to a problem you can get further if you let go of words and use images. You can play with the images, talk with the images, and discover a new slant on your situation.

We both have found that collage making has been a vitally important element in our personal growth and healing. As therapists we recognize the similar goals of talk-therapy and expressive arts. Both are opportunities to change fundamental assumptions so you can approach life differently. Collage making can tap into your visual, auditory, and touch senses. Making use of all of our senses enhances our ability to see life from a broader perspective. Our contributors have made substantial comments about the impact their own collage discoveries have had on their mind, body and spirit.

Some physicians believe that creative art expression triggers a relaxation response, which positively impacts the immune system. In his book, *Creative Healing*, Dr. Mike Samuels says that research shows that a person in prayer, a person making art, and a person healing all have the same physiological responses in terms of brain wave patterns. Healing arts, he says, will be the new alternative medical therapy.

Creative art making is a time for focusing within and can take you to a quiet, confident, centered place. You will often experience a feeling of being focused and centered when you are creating collages.

Is Collage Making Like Guided Imagery?

No. Guided imagery (or creative visualization) uses images, but the images we create in our mind's eye can float away. When you put your images down on paper, or other surfaces, you can play with them, contemplate them, and they can speak to you revealing what they mean. When you physically create art, your collage becomes a tangible record of where you've been. It is always there to look at whenever you want.

The real voyage consists not in
seeking new landscapes but in having new eyes.
—Marcel Proust

A Word From Gale And Ginny

When we feel like making collages, we don't want to read much. We want to create something. We're ready for action. Therefore, we have kept our instructions brief so you can get started quickly.

We look forward to hearing about your collage making experiences, and invite you to share them with us. We would enjoy receiving a color copy of your collage and reading your accompanying story.

We recommend following up with a licensed mental health practitioner if thoughts and feelings which emerge from this work seem to call for additional exploration or support. This book is not intended as a substitute for professional psychotherapy.

With affection,
Gale and Ginny

The authors lead workshops for the public and train therapists.
They can be contacted at
butterfly@lisco.com

The intuitive mind is a sacred gift and the rational mind a faithful servant.
We have created a society that honors the servant and has forgotten the gift.

—Albert Einstein

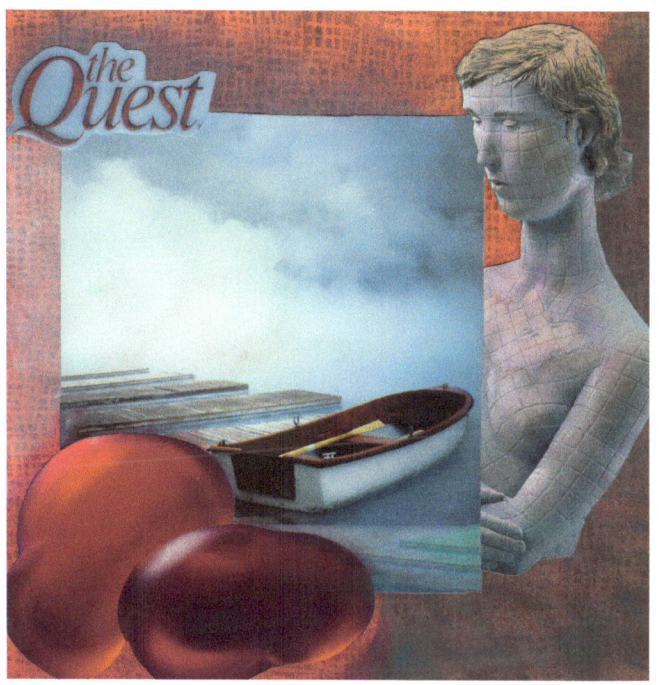

The trail is the thing, not the end of the trail.
Travel too fast and you miss all you are traveling for.
—Louis L'Amour, Ride the Dark Trail

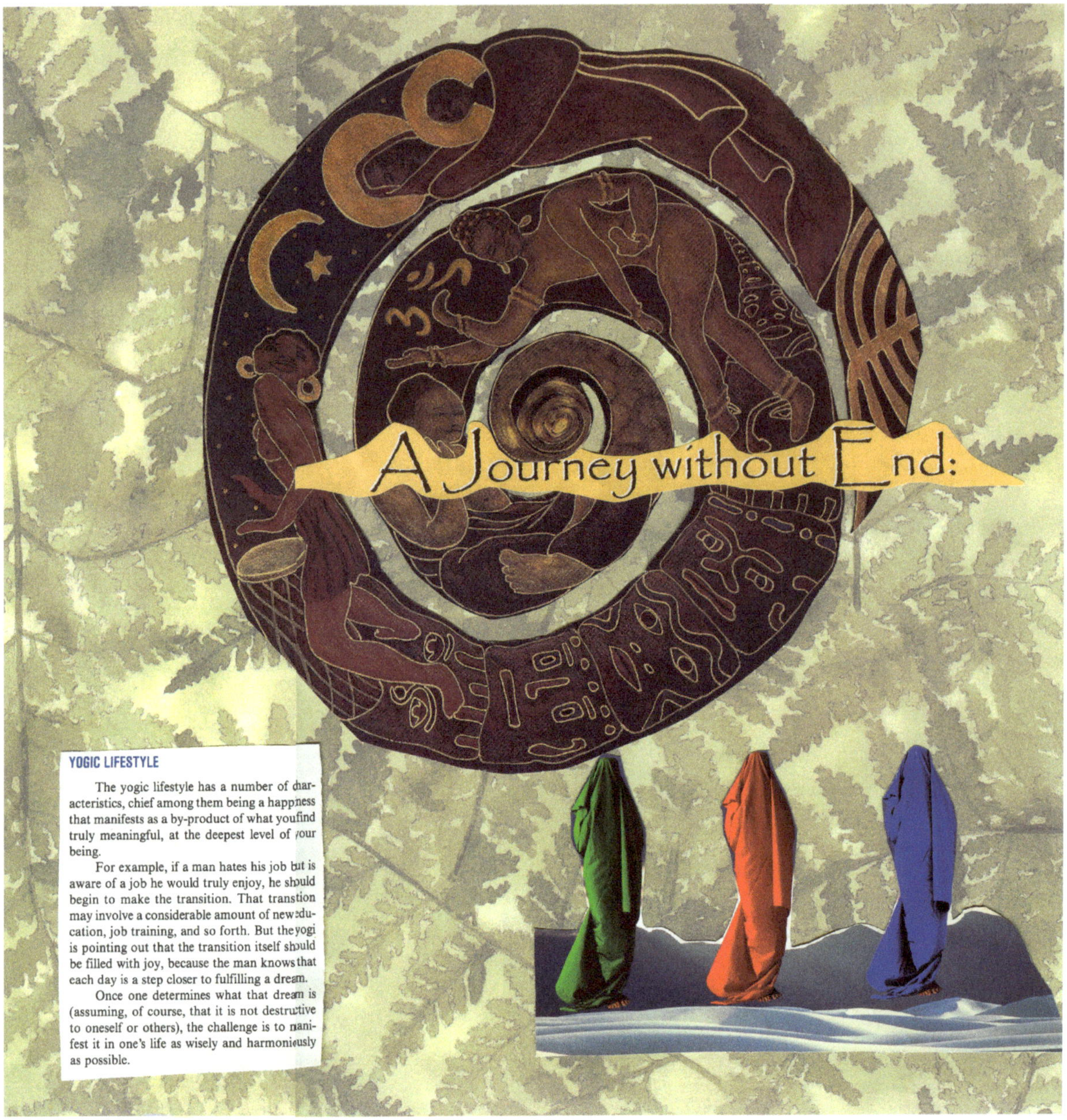

> **YOGIC LIFESTYLE**
>
> The yogic lifestyle has a number of characteristics, chief among them being a happiness that manifests as a by-product of what you find truly meaningful, at the deepest level of your being.
>
> For example, if a man hates his job but is aware of a job he would truly enjoy, he should begin to make the transition. That transition may involve a considerable amount of new education, job training, and so forth. But the yogi is pointing out that the transition itself should be filled with joy, because the man knows that each day is a step closer to fulfilling a dream.
>
> Once one determines what that dream is (assuming, of course, that it is not destructive to oneself or others), the challenge is to manifest it in one's life as wisely and harmoniously as possible.

—Image from Gale's 2006 Collage Calendar

Women in Saris Speak:

*We stand here covered in beautiful colors
facing the unknown.*

We have each other.

Yet we also support ourselves as well.

*We appear tranquil, perhaps resolved to
handle whatever we must.*

Make time to be still.

CHAPTER ONE

Making Your Collage

Collecting, Cutting, Gluing And Expressing

You must give birth to your images.
They are the future waiting to be born.

—Rainer Maria Rilke

Anything Goes

For some of us, early art experiences left us feeling self-conscious and anxious about using art materials. If this is true for you, relax and remember that school is over and that there are no rules for creating expressive art collage. Anything goes! You can scribble on your collage or even make a mess. Your cats can be purple and your people can be green. Give yourself permission to enjoy playing and experimenting with the materials.

Be assured that something helpful will emerge every time you sit down to make a collage. Just get started and see what happens. Let your hands do what they want. Let your heart guide your work. Follow your intuition and go with what feels right for you. Whatever you create at any time will be exactly what you need to do.

Notice what you are thinking and feeling as you are making your collage. Ideas and insights which come to you while you are working may be just as important as what you create or what you may learn from looking at your final product. Your finished collage may be complex or very simple. Either is fine. Both will give you important information.

Some collages are constructed in one sitting. You may want to work on other collages over a longer period of time. Those created in a short time can be a meaningful expression of your feelings or concerns and can lead to great learning. Sometimes you'll find the more time you take, the deeper the work and greater your insights will be.

Gathering Your Materials

Collect a variety of magazines and other craft materials like feathers and sparkles. Have your scissors and glue or tape nearby. You can mount your collected materials on paper, cardboard, a page in your journal, newspaper, a piece of wood, or anything else you want to use. Some people like to make their collages while sitting at a table and others prefer to work on the floor.

Some of Ginny's favorite images came from magazines which contained only one or two illustrations. You never know where your favorite images may be hiding.

Later on, you might consider inviting a group of friends to gather to make collages together. See Appendix A for some ideas on doing this.

See Appendix B for information on additional craft supplies.

Setting The Mood

Before beginning your collage, take the time to create some boundaries between the everyday busyness of your life and a more focused, meditative atmosphere. You can set the mood by lighting candles, playing soft background music, moving to a quiet room, sitting out on a sunny porch, or even under a shade tree. Focus on your surroundings. Listen to the nearby sounds. Take a few gentle breaths. Spend a few minutes thinking about what you're feeling, what you need, what's bothering you, what's on your mind and what you want right now.

Making Your Collage

Sort through the magazines for images that catch your eye. Work quickly. You don't need to understand anything about the images you've selected to use. Trust yourself to find the images you need to express your ideas. You may notice an occasional word or phrase that you want to use. Cut or tear out things until you feel finished. Choose the other materials you wish to add to your collage. You may try several different arrangements on your base before gluing or taping things into place. Remember to occasionally notice what you're thinking and feeling as you're working.

Getting To Know Your Collage

After you complete your collage, or feel like you are at a stopping point, take a quiet moment to just sit with your collage and take it in as a whole. What story do your images tell? Allow a word or words to emerge or pop into your mind to represent a title for your collage. Words that emerge spontaneously often give you other clues about what your collage is saying to you. If no title emerges, that's okay. Not every collage can be described in words. And some collages seem to be best left untitled.

When you have finished your collage, you may feel satisfied with the theme you've explored and the feelings you have expressed. You may feel you've completed whatever it was you needed to do. You can stop right there. Congratulations on your collage! You can always go back later and explore your collage further if you choose to do so.

Insights Over Time

Even though you may feel finished with your collage, hang it somewhere where you can look at it occasionally. Collages have a way of revealing further insights over time. Sometimes what may have seemed obvious at the time the collage was created looks different in hindsight. Feel free to add to or change your collage at any time.

Techniques For Further Exploration

In each chapter we will give you ideas for exploring the deeper levels of your collage. As you become more comfortable with the collage making process, you can choose the techniques you like the best.

If you want to begin to dig deeper now, here are some simple ways to start. As you look at your collage you may not know why you've selected a particular image, except that it was begging for your attention. Finding meaning in the images selected and the collage as a whole may be new to you. The following questions were designed to assist you in understanding your collage. There are no right or wrong answers to these questions. Choose the questions which seem to stimulate your thinking.

Diving Deeper

1. How did it feel for you to make your collage? If you haven't used art materials in a while, how did it feel to use them again? If you were feeling anxious at the start, how did you help yourself move past your anxiety?

2. How do you feel when you look at your collage? What do these feelings tell you about yourself and your life now?

3. Describe your process of constructing your collage. For example, are you messy, neat, spontaneous, organized, or relaxed? Does that style work for you? Do you approach life in the same way in which you approached your collage?

4. What story do your images tell? Are there several stories here?

5. Which images remain a mystery? What don't you understand yet?

6. What do you notice now that you didn't notice while you were making this collage?

7. Does it feel complete? If not, what do you need to add or perhaps remove?

8. What was the biggest surprise?

9. What did you learn? How can you use this information?

10. What would the next collage be if you made another one to expand on the theme of this one or tell the next part of the story? How would you change this collage? Could you take it apart and reassemble it to show the next part of the story? Could you remove or add images to the collage?

11. Which part of the collage draws your attention to it? Which part repels? How can you befriend an image that repels you? Ask this part of the collage to give you a positive or hopeful message about your situation.

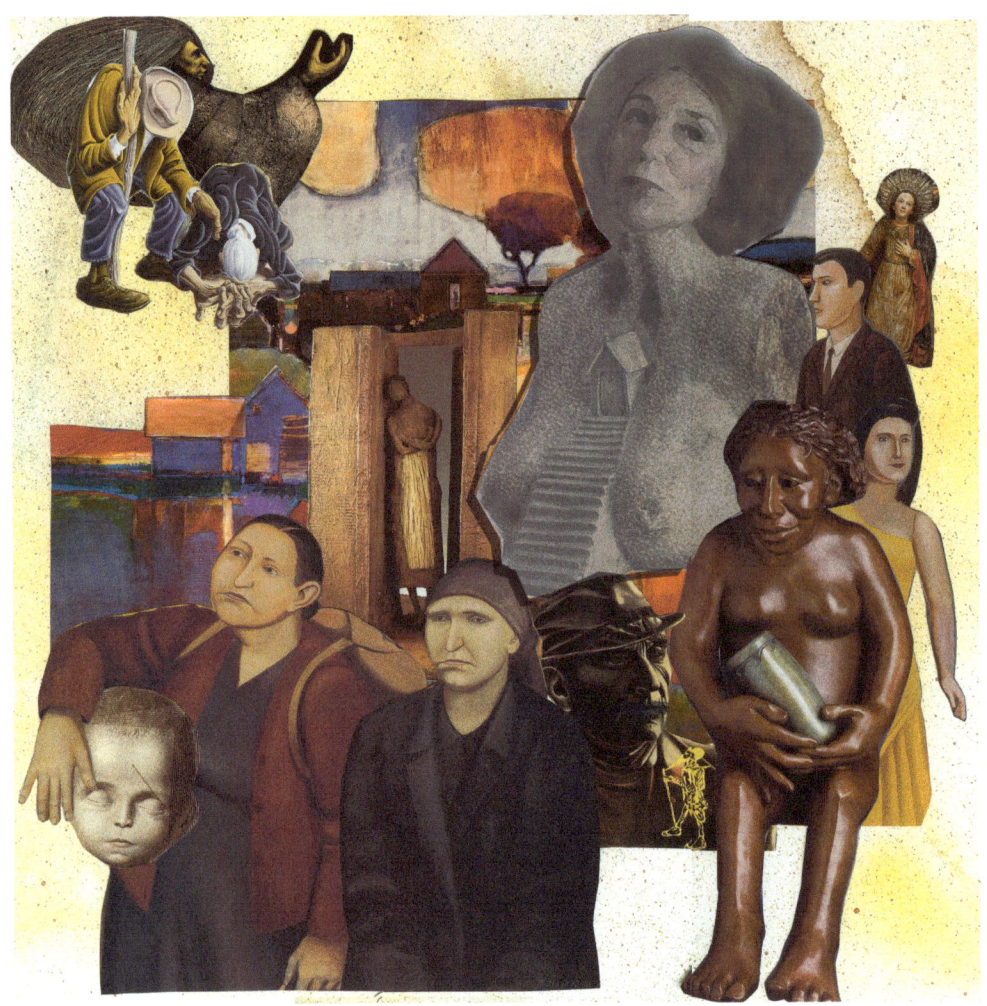

The Guest House

This being human is a guest house.

Every morning a new arrival—
A joy, a depression, a meanness—
Some momentary awareness comes
as an unexpected visitor.

Welcome and entertain them all
Even if they are a crowd of sorrows
Who violently sweep your house
empty of its comforts.

Still, treat each guest honorably.
He may be cleaning you out for some new delight.

The dark thought, the shame, the malice—
Meet them at the door laughing and invite them in.

Be grateful for whoever comes
Because each has been sent as a guide from beyond.

Welcome difficulty.

Learn the alchemy True Human Beings know:
The moment you accept what troubles
you have been given, the door opens.

Welcome difficulty as a familiar comrade.

Joke with torment brought by the friend.

Sorrows are the rags of old clothes
and jackets that serve to cover
and then are taken off.

That undressing
and the beautiful naked body underneath,
is the sweetness that comes after grief.

—Rumi

  Butterfly At Daybreak

CHAPTER TWO

Capturing A Sense Of Self

Releasing Feelings, Solving Problems, Moving Forward

An artist is not a special kind of person,
but every person is a special kind of artist.

—Ananda Coomaraswamy

Your collage will capture who you are in pictures and help you focus quickly on your current life and present needs. Creating collages with a topic in mind can lead you to new insights and a greater self-awareness. For example, let's say you want to make a collage about some feelings that you are experiencing. As you are working, the images you are selecting begin to absorb the intensity of your feelings. These feelings are then released as opposed to staying locked up inside.

Perhaps this is a challenging time in your life and you want to make a collage to look for a solution. By constructing a collage you can see clearly, in visual language, what your challenge looks like. Now it is easier to understand and easier to figure out what to do next.

In this chapter you will learn a technique called Conversing With Your Collage. You will learn how to talk to your images and listen as they speak with you. You will call forth your deepest wisdom and intuition, and become your own best source of information.

The way to get started is by taking stock of yourself at the moment—right here—right now.

Take a few minutes and ask yourself some questions like:

- How am I feeling right now?
- What am I missing or needing today?
- Am I upset, but can't seem to find the words to describe it?
- What challenges am I facing?
- Am I reacting to a stressful situation?
- What are my burning questions?
- Am I missing an opportunity to play?

Once you've asked yourself some of these questions, look at the following topics and pick the one that appeals to you.

Seeing My Life Now

Look for images, which capture the "right here, right now" of your life, images which tell the story of your life at the present moment. This collage may help you stand back far enough from your busy life to see more clearly what is really happening.

Knowing My Feelings

Select images which illustrate your present feelings whether mad, sad, upset, depressed, or anxious and so on. Remember that gratitude, contentment, and joy are also feelings. How have you been feeling lately?

Facing Challenges

If a current challenge or obstacle has you feeling stuck, portray this challenge or obstacle in images the best you can. Then converse with your images as we describe later in this chapter. Ask each image to suggest a practical or creative solution to your current challenge.

Answering Burning Questions

Sometimes questions hound us until we find the answer. "What's my life purpose?" "What is my spiritual path?" "What career would best suit me?" "What kind of partner do I want?" What is your burning question? Collage your question and ask your images for some answers.

Finding What's Missing

At times you may know what is missing from your life, but you're not clear on how to get it. Sometimes you may sense that something is missing, but you can't pinpoint what it is. Find images of what's missing in your life or scan images until something pops out at you and tells you what is missing. Creating this collage can give you insights as to what you need to include in your life and conversing with your images can give you some ideas about how to do that.

Saying Something About Current Events And Global Issues

Sometimes current events and global issues are in the forefront of our minds. However, they may be under the surface of our awareness, troubling and affecting how we act on a daily basis. Think about an issue that's been on your mind—a poem, a newspaper article, or something you saw on TV. Have your collage make a statement about that issue and/or feelings that were stirred up. Ask your images how you might help to change this situation. Or make a collage showing your vision of a healthier community and/or planet.

Finding Comfort And Energy

Comfort is a necessity in a busy life. Choose images that bring a feeling of comfort or energy when you look at them. Your images may be of outdoor or indoor settings. Arrange your images into a collage and place it where you can view it when your spirit needs a lift or when you need help to unwind and go to sleep after a busy day. The simple act of making a collage can be comforting!

Making Time For Play And Relaxation

We need playtime to balance out our responsibilities and restore our energy. Make a collage which reflects your playful spirit or brings a smile to your face. Play around with some of the craft materials mentioned in Appendix B and pretend that you're five years old again. Have FUN. This will cultivate some energy for further work.

For yet deeper exploration, we highly recommend the technique presented below called Conversing With Your Collage. Many collages presented throughout this book contain examples of this technique.

Conversing With Your Collage

Ask an image from your collage to describe itself. For example, if you chose an image of a bridge, **imagine you are the bridge and describe yourself.**

Then pick up your pencil and write down what the bridge is saying. Don't worry about grammar, punctuation or spelling. For example, you might start by writing, "I am Mary's bridge. I am close to the water below me and somewhat rickety," and finish the description. You may write one sentence, one paragraph, or one page. We have discovered that the description of your image usually describes you in some way. Just play with this process and see what happens.

Then ask an image in your collage to give you some words of wisdom or advice about your life right now or any other subject on which you would like some feedback. For example, you might write, "I am Mary's bridge. I would advise you to…." Obviously these are only stream-of-consciousness thoughts and no one would ever follow the suggestions without careful assessment. However, we have often received affirmations from our images as to our strengths and talents, or information which has shed light or understanding on a current situation. In any case, all of the feedback from our images has been helpful, sometimes even humorous! Some of the collages shown in this book include conversations the collage maker carried on with the images.

Here's another example. If you chose an image of a cat, ask your cat to describe itself. Then pick up a pencil and write down the first thoughts that come to mind. You might start by writing, "I am Mary's cat. I am short-haired, yellow-eyed, independent, resourceful, and love to sleep. I do what I want and don't take orders from anyone!" Consider how the cat's description of itself is similar or dissimilar to who you are. Next, ask your cat to give you some words of wisdom. If you were asking your cat how best to support your health, your cat might say,

"Take care to get all the sleep you need. This is not a luxury, it's a necessity. It's hard to be creative without enough sleep. And be open to other people's assistance and words of wisdom. One can be too independent at times."

If we were asking our cat for help in publishing our book, our cat might say, "This stuff is great. Just get it out there. Don't lose any sleep worrying about it."

Now look at the image doing the talking. Use its present circumstance to describe itself. For example, the cat might say, "I sit here squeezed between the image of a man and slightly behind a flower." The conversation can include how it feels to be positioned that way or how it feels to be draped with cloth or how it feels about where it's sitting. It can be surprising to see how informative this can be.

You can continue to converse with every image in your collage.

Notice also the placement of an image on the edges of the page.

Does the image have room to fully express itself or has it run out of room to breathe? We encourage collage makers to ignore the edges of the paper and to allow images to expand, if they choose to do so. You can also explore an image which seems too crowded along the edge of the paper. For example, a tree which is only partially represented and/or crowded along the top edge of the page may be saying, "I need more room to grow. I'm feeling stifled. I'm crowded. Let me expand. Don't limit my growth. I can do more than this. I'm capable of greater achievement. Why are you stopping me from growing?"

Some other questions you can ask your images are:

- What feelings am I experiencing in this situation? Are there feelings that I am trying to suppress?
- What do I need to release or let go of?
- What is my best course of action for the future? (If one is called for)
- What do I need first?
- What other questions do I need to ask?

Writing With Your Non-Dominant Hand

You might also try writing with your non-dominant hand. This helps you slow down enough to help you tap into your quiet, inner wisdom. Using your non-dominant hand may feel awkward to you at first but we have found that everyone can manage. It doesn't matter if anyone else can read your writing because only you need to know what you have written. You can also set up a conversation between images by using your right hand to represent one image and your left hand to represent the other image. You could spend weeks or even months getting to know your collage.

Occasionally people find their intuitive thoughts coming so quickly that they're not able to write quickly enough with their non-dominant hand to record their thoughts as they come. In such cases, you may want to switch back to your dominant hand and catch up on your thoughts. Some people find, however, that continuing to write with the non-dominant hand is worth the effort and elicits deeper feedback from the image in question.

Gale always uses her dominant hand when writing. Ginny finds that using her non-dominant hand is helpful. For her, writing the first few words are usually the most difficult part of the process. Once she gets started the words seem to flow.

Lucia Capacchione has written an entire book on the use of the non-dominant hand, *The Power of Your Other Hand.* It's a good resource, particularly for conversing with one's inner child.

It's Up To You

Choose the topic that attracts you and catches your interest right now, and begin creating a collage with pictures and words related to your topic. Let the images find you. Be open to what attracts your attention. Remember, anything goes!

You can't use up creativity.
The more you use, the more you have.

—Maya Angelou

It's Not A Laughing Matter

When an acquaintance offered to tell me the latest battered-woman joke I felt rage inside of me. I was too upset to sleep that night, so I started working on this collage to calm myself down. Just putting my feelings into images on paper seemed to help.

The rock wall represents all the barriers women have encountered in their quest for equality, including homes safe from violence. The spotted leopards represent my anger. I was ready to chew up this guy and spit him out in pieces. The butterfly represents the transformation of violence into peace.

I worked on the collage for several days before I was totally able to let go of the incident.

—Alice, 50's

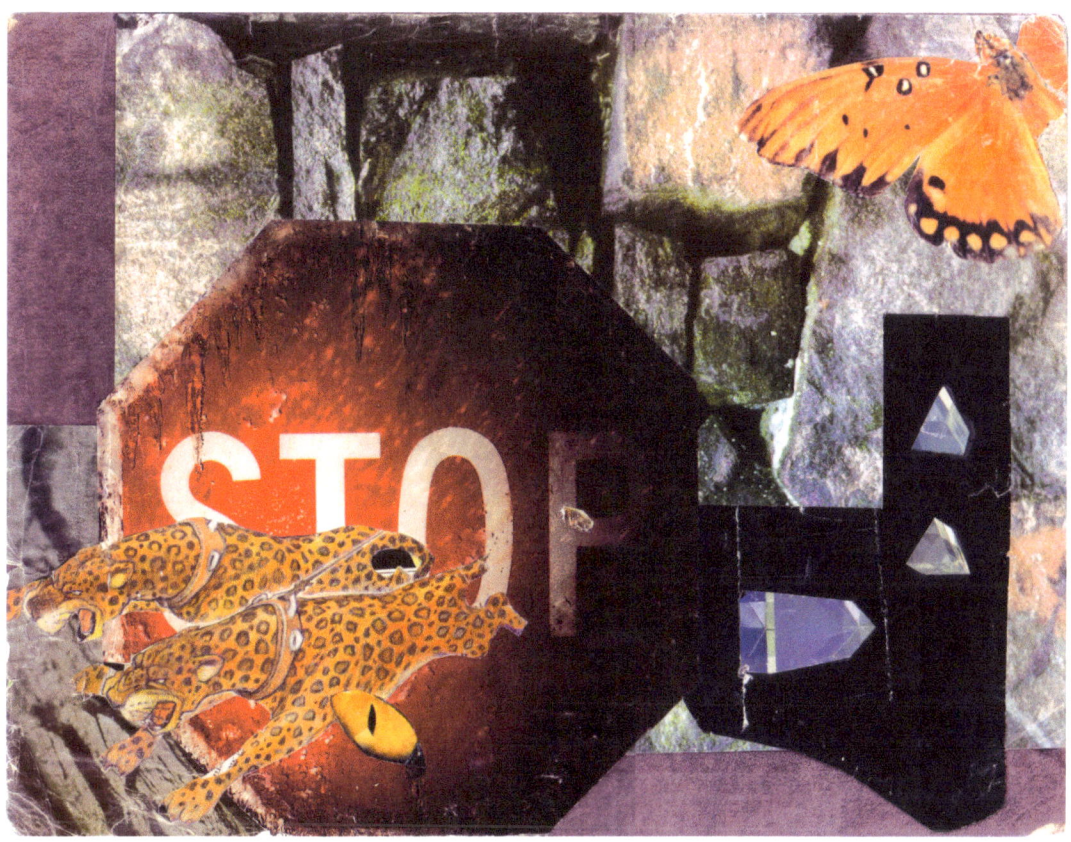

Butterfly Speaks To Alice:

I am Alice's butterfly. I rise above conflict. Alice, your power is in your anger. Don't let anyone take it from you. Stand your ground with this issue. It's not a laughing matter. Men are afraid that if women take back the power which is their own, that men will have nothing. That view lacks insight into the true nature of the world and the possibility of partnership between men and women.

Leopards Speak To Alice:

Alice, check out your own tendency toward rage. You could hurt someone physically with your anger. What's right for the gander is also right for the goose.

A Small Golden Door

This piece was done several years ago. It was a time for contemplating change. I found myself focused on doors and doorways and windows of all kinds.

There were a variety of construction materials offered to work with and three-dimensionality intuitively fit the subject. My outer door represents life's fullness to the point of excess: food with no restraint, lavish surroundings and decadent sexuality. Within these doors waits a dim future of deprivation and decay with some glimmers of hope. Within the last small golden door, a black mystery.

—Carole, 50's

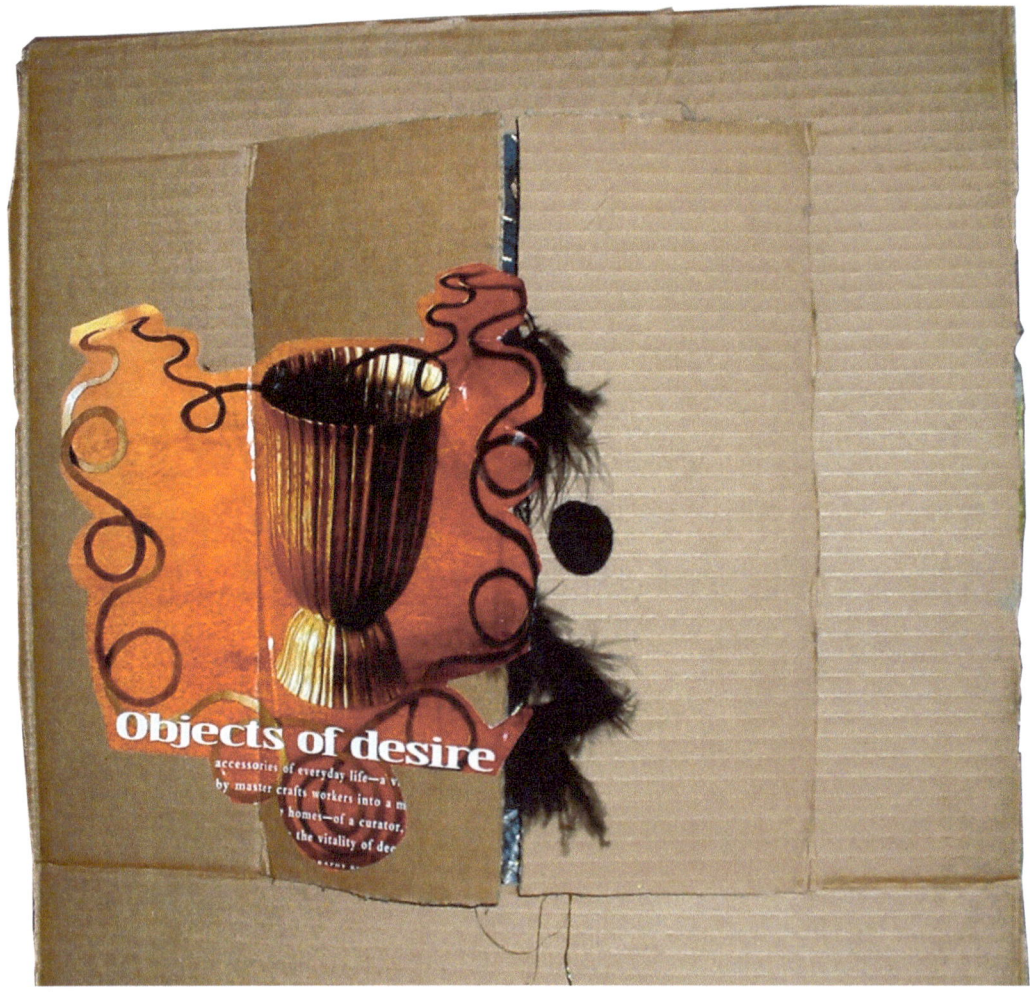

Outer Door Speaks To Carole:

I am here for you only as a memory now. No longer are you free to experience me in bursts of immoderation. Your libido is dulled and your cholesterol is too high for chocolate without guilt. I am a reminder of your losses.

Inner Scene Speaks To Carole:

Is there any fun left for me? Must I always be careful to eat right and visit the dentist endlessly? In the end I will age and become fragile. How will I enjoy life?

The Inside Of The Small Gold Box Speaks To Carole:

I am mystery. The unknown. The future. I am compact, quiet and safe. You may or may not rest easy in me. I am inevitable.

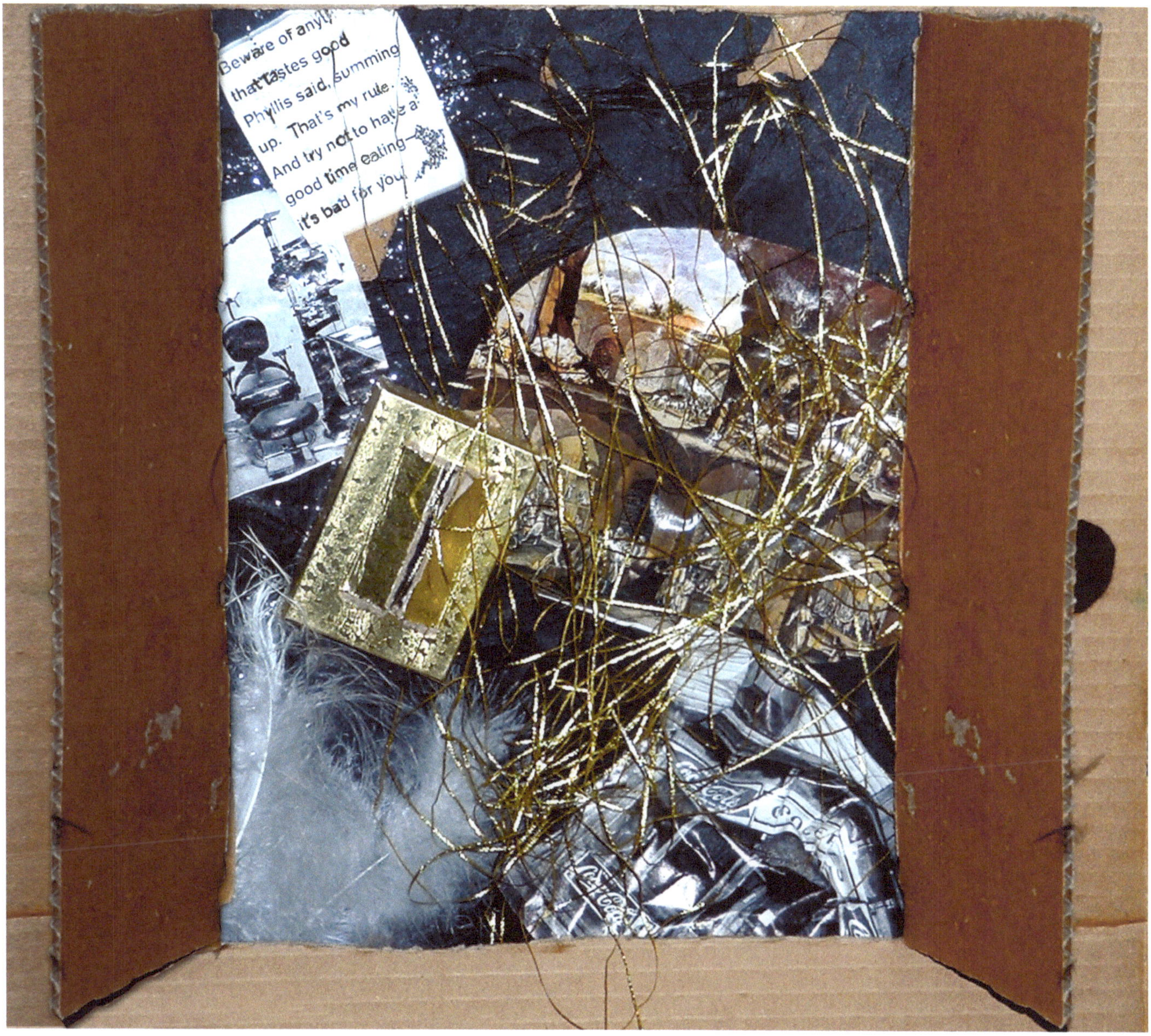

Completing The Puzzle

After trying to meditate on a current theme in my life I realized how distracted I was. I headed to the magazines. Images that attracted me got pulled from their binding with no thoughts of my connection to my present situation. I wanted to possess these beautiful and dramatic images. I suspended my quest for meaning as I arranged, cut and pasted four separate collages. Finally, I put them together as I would a puzzle, looking for the best fit. Then I spoke to each part to see what the images might reveal to me.

—Yvonne, 60's

Yvonne, Speaking To The Woman With Headdress In The Lower Left:

I am most attracted to you. You are the peace and tranquility I seek. You are simplicity and beauty.

To The Confident Man With Sneakers:

You straddle two worlds. Your open legs dominate my life. I question my values as I face my losses. Always a younger, nurturing woman nearby to remind you of your importance. I, on the other hand, need to endlessly remind myself that I am still worthy. Perhaps you earned your place by being responsible, wise and giving. I doubt it.

To The Woman With Mask And Lace:

You must constantly face the decision to remain hidden or to show yourself. I think it would be easier to take the risk to unmask.

To The Woman In Sneakers:

Tell me your secret. How do you persevere? How can I learn to endure the strenuous?

To The City:

You are so interesting, so busy. Novelty at every turn. You are my seducer.

To The Pictures On The Walls:

You are my history.

Indeed my collage had presented me with my current life themes: balancing, aging, self-worth as a retired person, whether to be open about my vulnerability, the value of the past and long-term relationships, the ever-lurking seducer with new and interesting opportunities to take me off my chosen path.

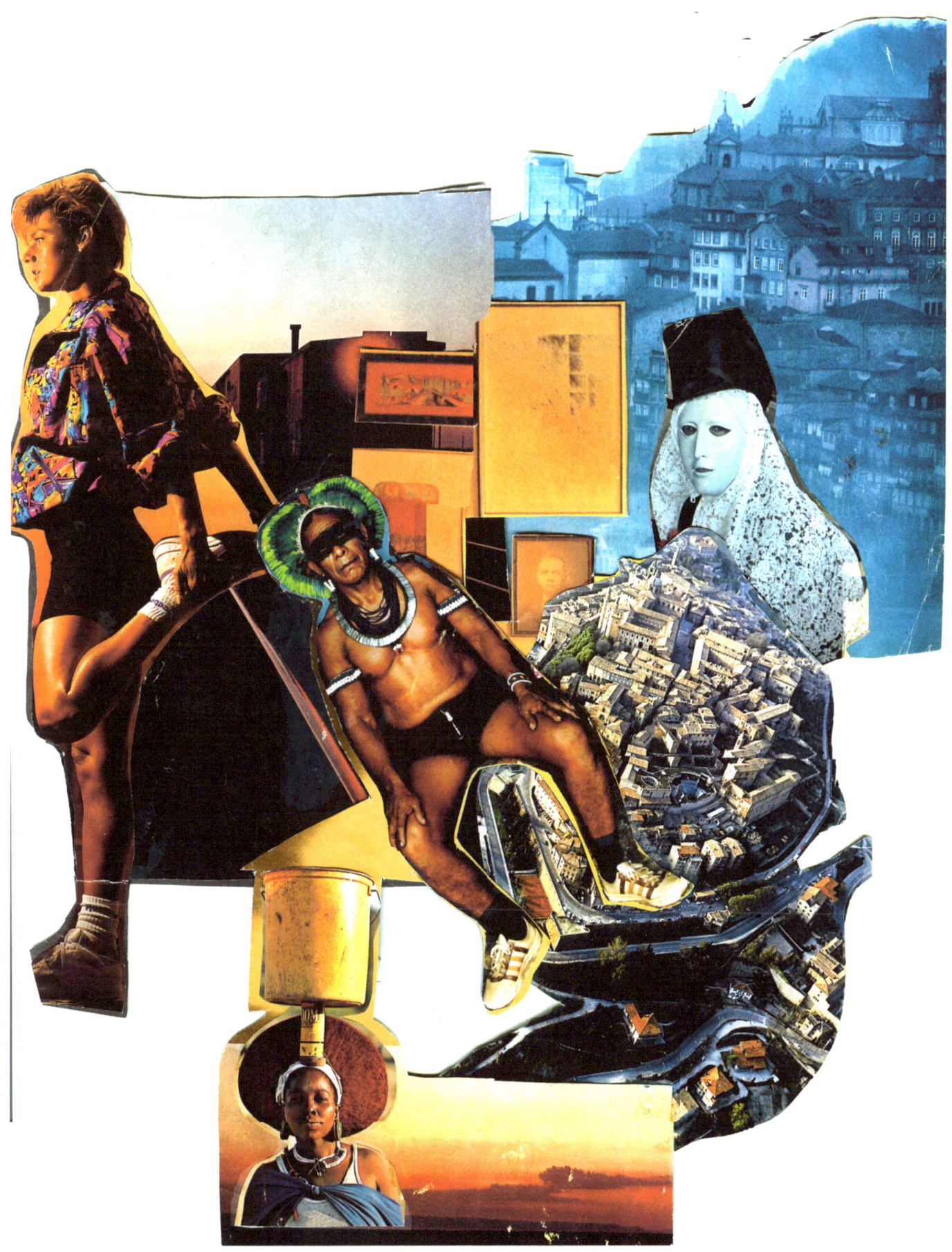

Waiting For My Reward

Journal entry one day before collage was constructed: "I am in a spiritual void or on a plateau. I have stopped my seeking, for God and for a man. I'm resting. I curl up in the comfort of my corner nest by morning and nestle into the coziness of my bed with fiction by night. I am not journeying forth. How long do I wait for the energy to strike me? And then, where to go, what to do, what to seek?"

—Nancy, 60's

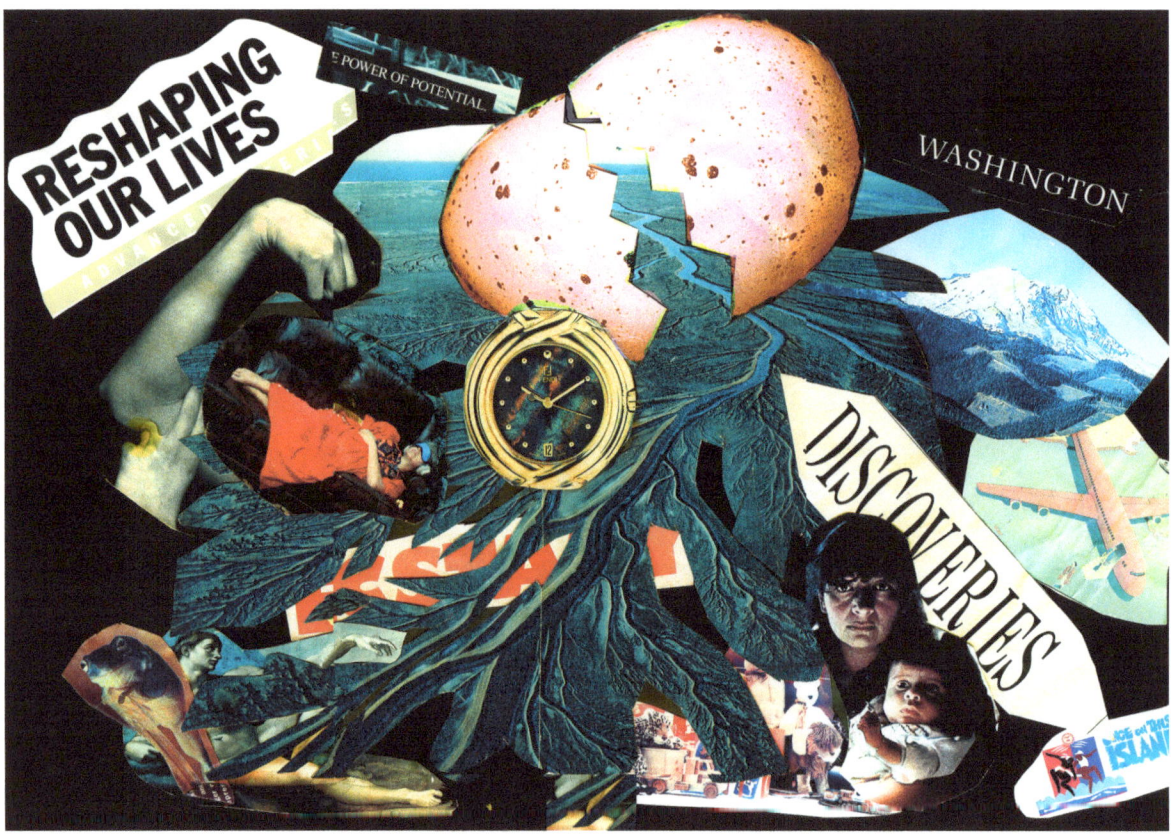

Nancy Speaks To The Sleeping Figure:

Why are you sleeping? What are you waiting for?

Figure Speaks To Nancy:

I've done all this work on myself and now I am waiting for my reward. My shell has cracked open. I've taken many paths and have had great pleasure, but passion, ecstasy, playfulness, abandon, I am missing. Time is running out. I want something to grab me and I don't want to do the work to wake up my body, to wake up my soul.

Architects Of Time

As far as I'm concerned, the Native Americans have a healthier view of time than do more so-called sophisticated cultures such as ours. I use this collage with two large figures of Seminole elders and the large figure of an Easter Island monolith, to remind me that I can get so busy staying on schedule that I can lose track of what's really important to me. When I look down on the earth from afar I remember the larger picture; that time is relative and that I can live my life at a pace that is truly healthy for my body, mind and spirit. I may have to give up some things to do this, but I do have a choice.

—Rae, 50's

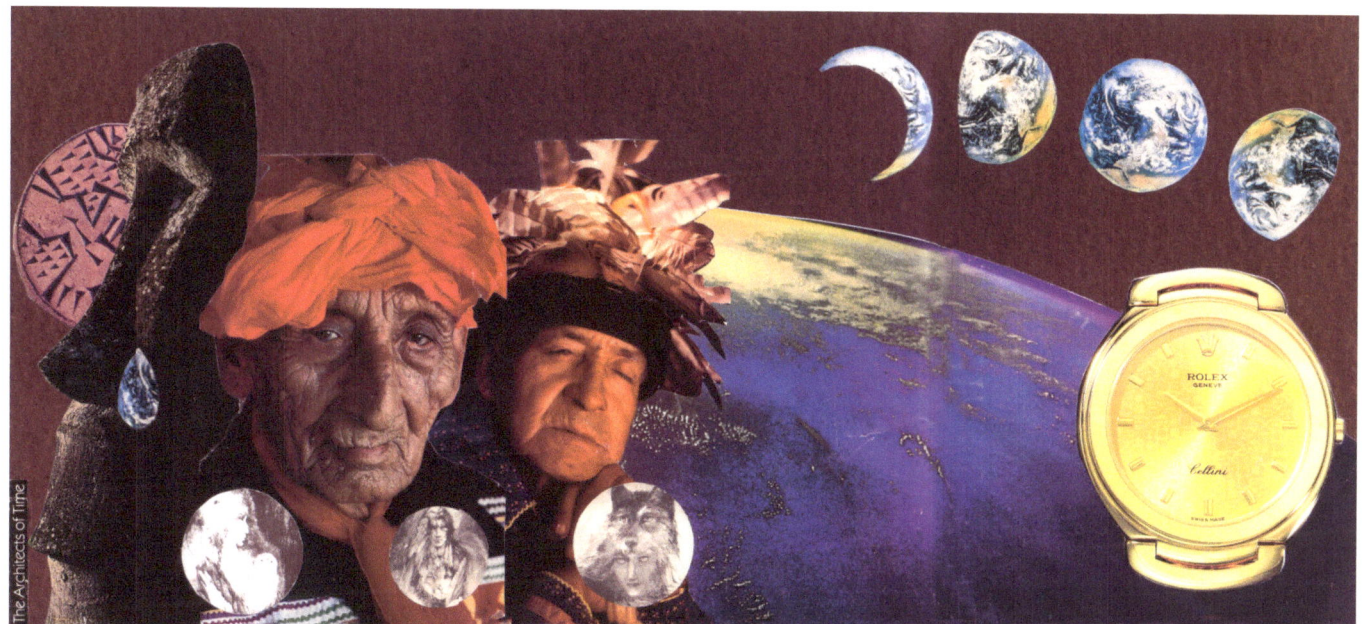

The Architects of Time

The Easter Island Monolith Speaks To Rae:

The tear on my cheek represents my sorrow that many humans have lost their awareness of the natural pulse of the universe. Synchronize your pulse with nature and you will find greater joy. When your nose is stuck in all of the details, real life passes you by! Stop your rushing and be with time, not on time.

Undoing The Damage

This collage expresses my sadness at the damage being done to our environment.

The ballerina represents all of our grandchildren who will be inheriting our Earth.

—Alice, 50's

Earth Speaks To Alice:

The Earth will have its turn. All is not lost. Hope lives. Do your part. Keep tribal consciousness. Remember the circle!

Mouse Speaks:

Remember the little things. We count! Pay attention to the details!

Butterfly Speaks:

Soar like the Eagle. Get the view from above. God remains hopeful.

Dolphin Speaks:

I can help you heal!

Octopus Speaks:

My tears of hope cleanse the skies and the water. Never give up. All is not lost, as long as there is a star in heaven, and don't I look like one!

Little Girl Speaks:

I'm the star here! Don't let me down. I won't have a leg to stand on! Fine thing to bring me here to this Earth, and then pull the rug out from under me! You should all be ashamed.

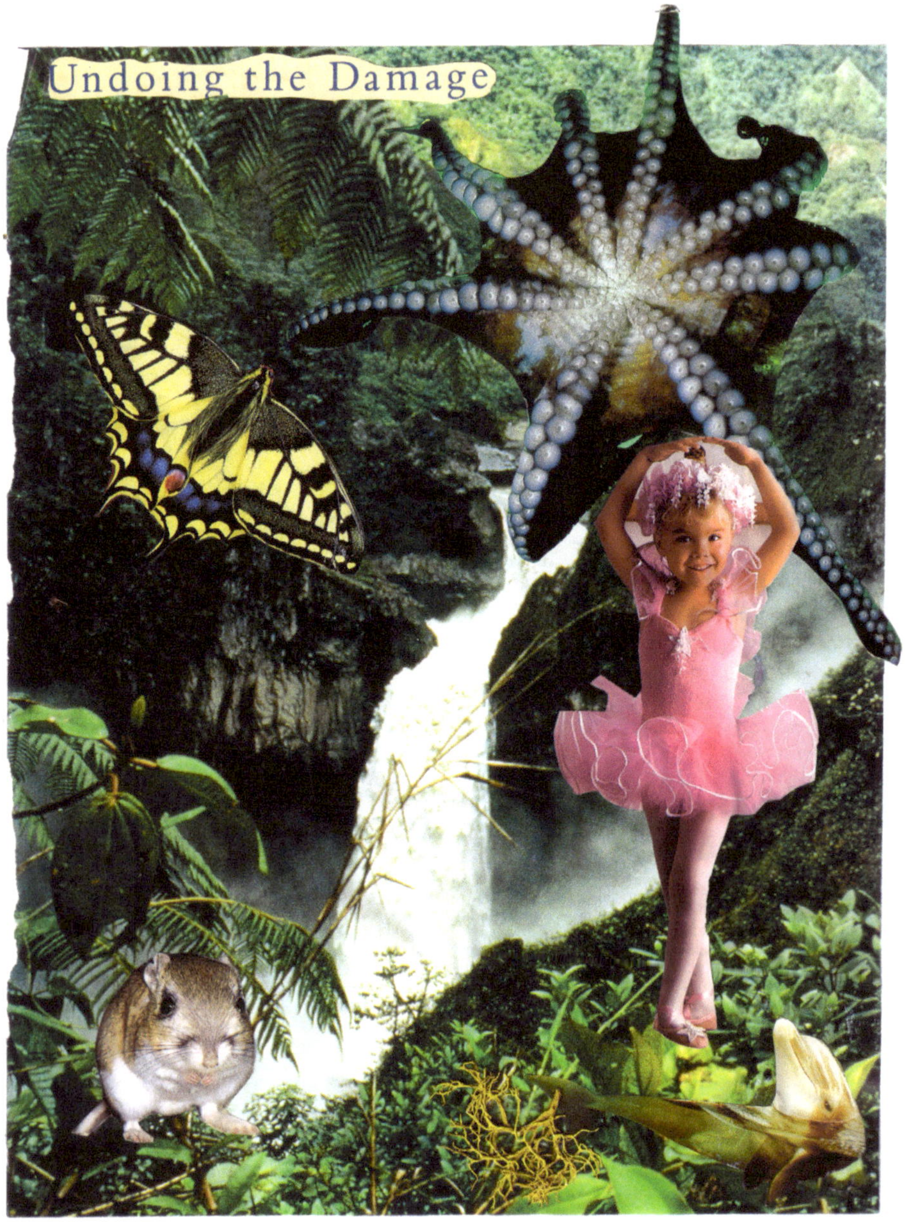

The Star In The Sky

On Mother's Day, Dad called to tell us that Mom was seriously ill following surgery. I packed my suitcase and flew off to Cape Cod. Mom died a week later. I was sad but relieved that she was now out of pain, and "flying free, spirit at peace."

I started this collage on my way to Cape Cod, using the airline's monthly magazine, and finished it back home, still using only one magazine.

The image at the bottom right represents Cape Cod where Mom and Dad lived for 25 years after Dad retired. Mom's name "Stella" means star. The airplane represents my journey to Cape Cod, knowing that this would probably be the last time I would see her alive. The airplane also represents my mom departing into the sunset.

I was amazed that all the images I found seemed especially pertinent. Making this collage helped me deal with my feelings of grief around Mom's death. Mom's words to me gave me the feeling that she is looking after me in spirit, if not in body.

—Ginny, 50's

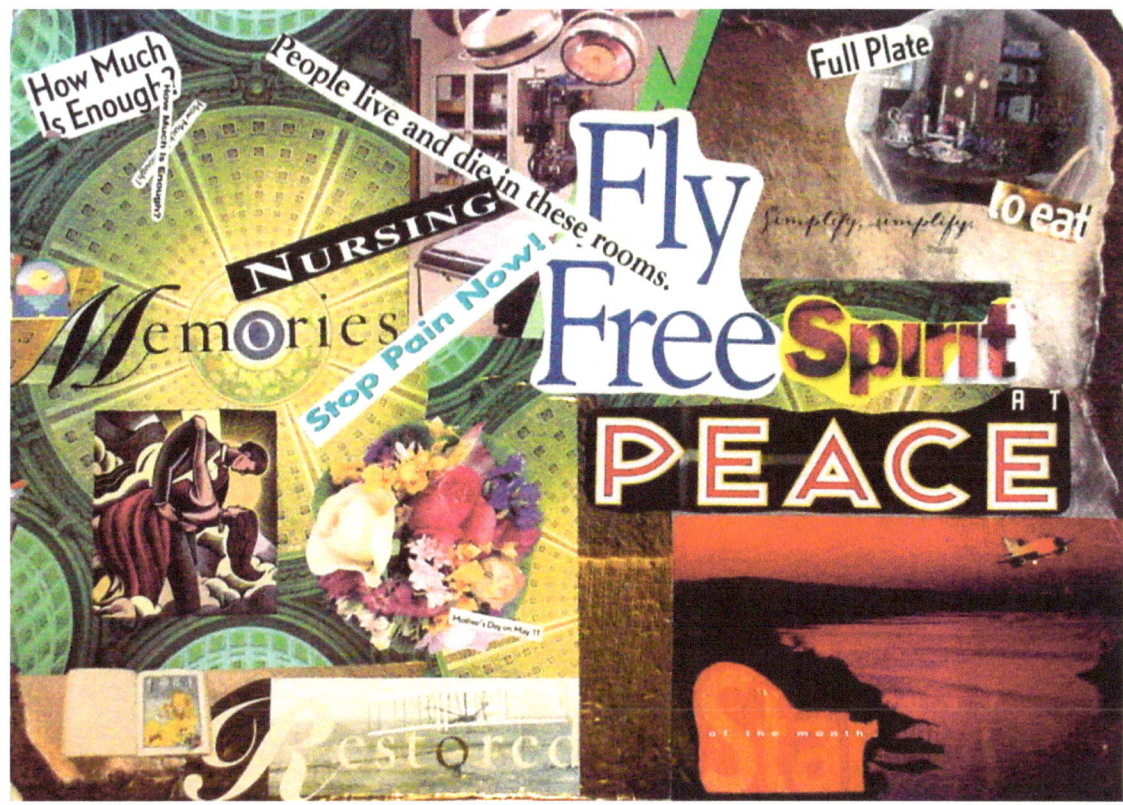

Airplane (speaking for and representing Mom) Speaks To Ginny:

I may be heading off into the sunset, but I am not leaving you! I am the star in the sky which you admire. My spirit is everywhere and my arms are around you at every moment, just as your arms were around me before I died. I do not need your tears. All is as before. I see your future and it is clear.

Interestingly, my Dad asked for a copy of the collage, which he framed and hung on the wall, and referred to it frequently as he grieved Mom's death.

Mandala: Circles Of Gratitude

Many ancient cultures have used circular forms for expressive and spiritual art including the Tibetan Buddhist sand-painters and Native American shieldmakers. The psychologist Carl Jung named these circles mandalas and believed the circular shape had a powerful effect on the maker of the mandala.

Mandalas serve the purpose of centering and focusing energy, releasing tension, calming ourselves and containing feelings. Some people see the circle as representing feminine energy and as a sacred space within which we can find a sense of wholeness and unity with life around us.

Making mandalas can be used as a ritual to begin or end the day.

I chose to focus my mandala on my feelings of gratitude.

As I searched for the images I wanted for my collage, many images seemed to choose me. As my mandala took an unexpected direction and began to take shape, feelings of thankfulness and love filled my heart. I realized, once more, why I often prefer to express myself with images instead of words.

I collect heart-shaped rocks and was thrilled to find the image which now rests in the center of my mandala! Once I had located my "center," it seems as if everything else fell into place.

—Ginny, 50's

I Am Grateful.

For the moon and her cycles and feminine energy,
For my hands which reach out for love and support,
For my heart which provides me with wisdom and guidance,
For the rock-solid Earth which grounds and supports me,
I am grateful.

—Ginny

At the still point, in the center of the circle, one can see the infinite in all things.

—Chuang Tzu

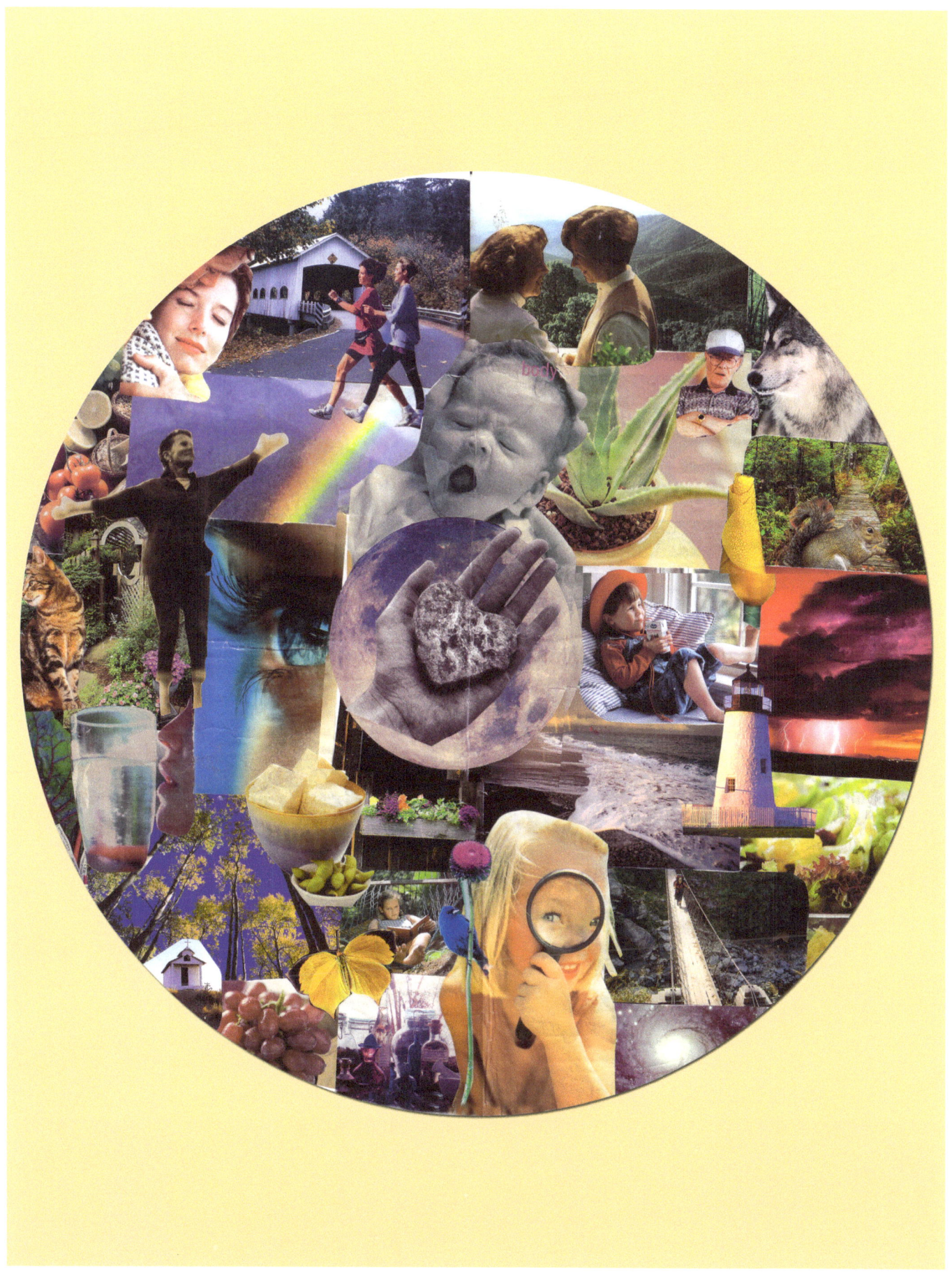

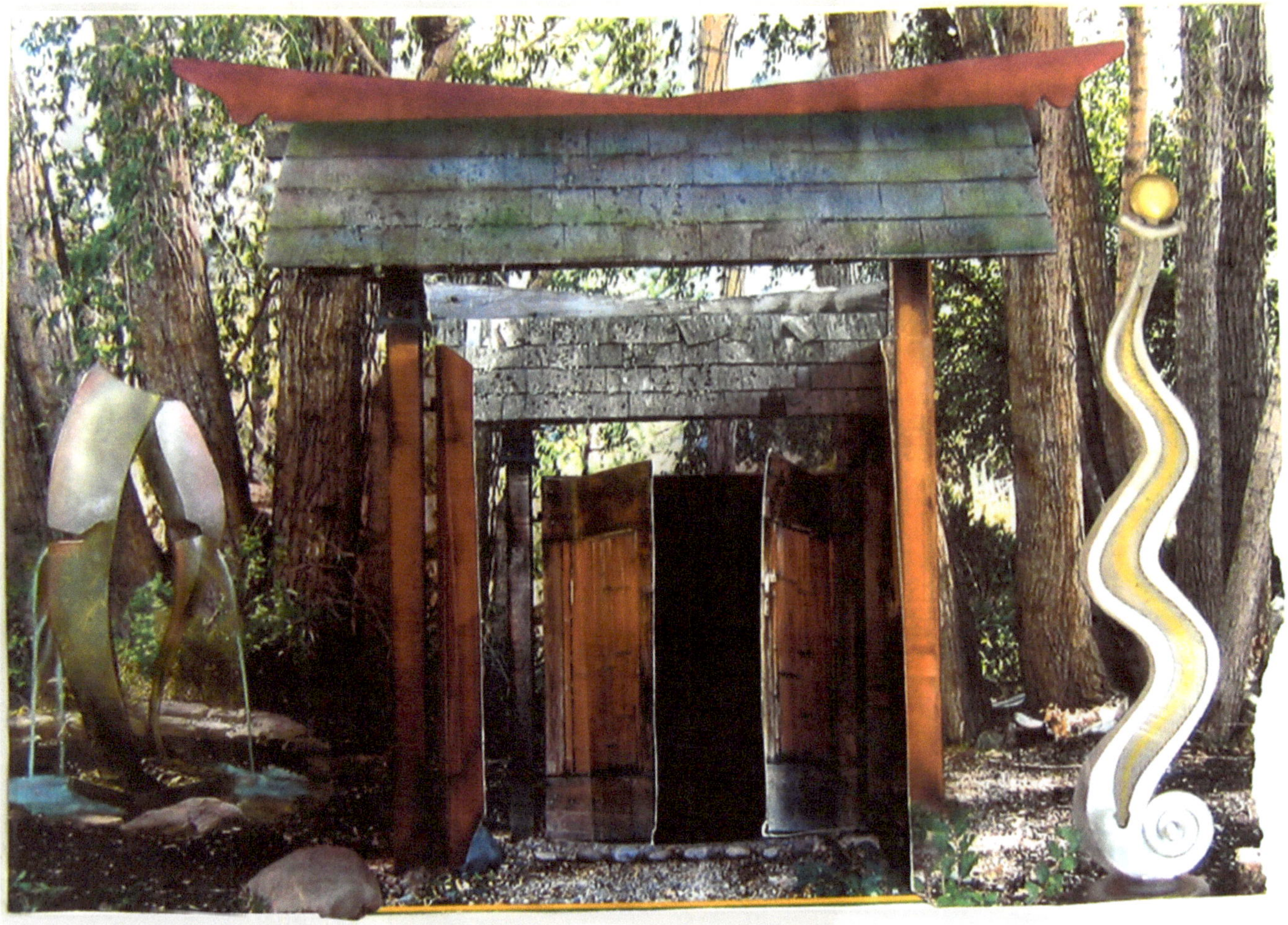

The only trust required is to know that
when there is one ending there will be another beginning.

—Clarissa Pinkola Estes

CHAPTER THREE

Exploring Your Past

Your Past Speaks To Your Present

*The whole life of a person is the slow trek to recover the two
or three simple images in whose presence his heart first moved.*

—Albert Camus

Have you ever said, "It's over, it's in the past, it doesn't affect who I am now"?

Like it or not, your history has shaped who you've become. To consciously choose to be the person you want to be requires taking a good look at what you learned as a child. Collaging is a great way to reconnect with your childhood. And sometimes it's fun just to go back and play.

A Mixture Of Memories

When you think about your past, you might find your memories traveling back toward hard times or good times. You learned things from both experiences.

Making a collage about a hard time can remind you of the strengths and resilience that helped you get through it. First capture in pictures the experience you are recalling. What are the feelings that this brings up? Capture those, too, if you can. Remember the people who helped. Recall some specific good that came out of it. What do you do well now that you learned to do from that experience?

Collaging about good times reminds you of your strengths and talents and the joy of having fun. These memories can help sustain you when you go through your next hard time. Good memories remind us all of the joy that is still alive in us. Try to capture your memories of a good time in pictures. What are the feelings that come to mind? Try to find images for those feelings. Enjoy these feelings again. What made this a good time? Be open to surprises.

Forgotten Memories

Sometimes playing with colorful art and craft materials can bring back the joy of childhood play and other memories long since forgotten. Rather than make a collage about your past, you might want to feel like a child again right now. Just start playing with images and materials. Create as a child would, with no intention at all. Notice how that feels to you. Do you need more of this in your life right now? How could you do that? Notice memories that come to the surface as you're working. Notice any change in your energy level, too.

Talking About Your Memories

After making your collage, converse with your images if you wish. (Review the section in Chapter 1 on Getting To Know Your Collage or review Chapter 2 on Conversing With Your Collage.) If you find that during or after working on your collage you have feelings that you want to talk more about, do that with a trusted friend.

How we remember,
and what we remember,
and why we remember,
form the most personal map of our individuality.

—Christina Baldwin,
author of Calling the Circle

We have stories
as old as the great seas
breaking through the chest
flying out the mouth,
noisy tongues that once were silenced,
all the oceans we contain
coming to light.

—Linda Hogan, Chickasaw

Pinwheel

Our class was asked to spend an hour playing with the art materials as young children might. I started out making a flower, then began thinking that the flower looked like a pinwheel. I remember that Mom would always buy me a pinwheel, and I would hold it out the window. My Dad was still alive and it was a happy time.

—Sharon, 40's

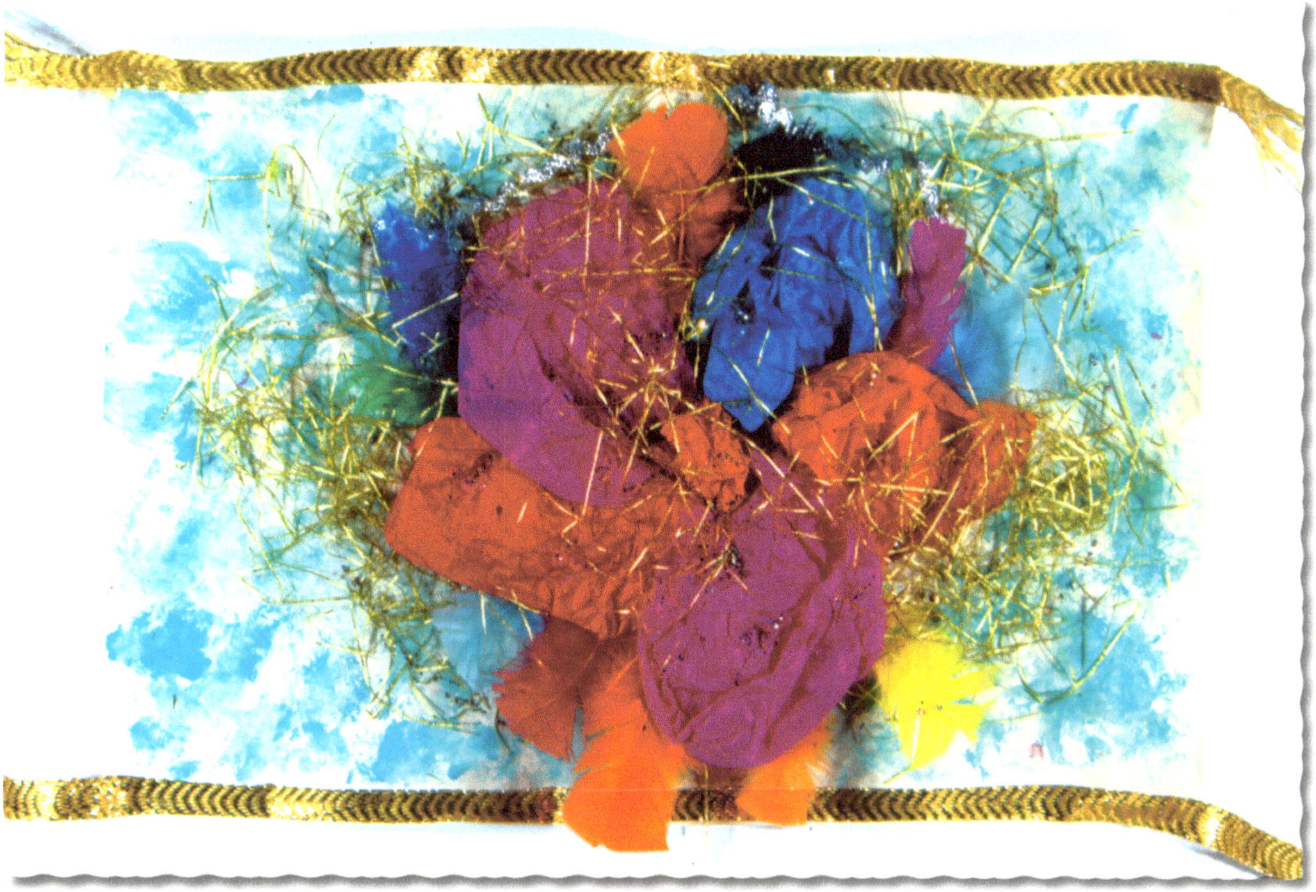

It's Never Too Late To Get Enough

This is a collage of my family: my mom, my dad and my younger sister.

My dad seemed to worry a lot, especially about being in the right place at the right time. Dad enjoyed athletics, and having two daughters and no sons, he gave us plenty of encouragement to participate. I was a long-legged runner and long-jumper but never succeeded in organized sports. I think he was probably disappointed about that. Mom seemed to be around to take care of our needs, including good nutrition. I was proud of the fact that she was a nurse, but she didn't go back to work as a nurse until I was in high school. She chose to define herself as a housewife. She said recently that she wished she'd gone back to work (outside the home) sooner. My sister and I loved to play and I especially loved to explore the outdoors, being very curious about the unknown. Mom and Dad supported us in enjoying some of the extras of childhood, such as taking music lessons. It seems that I lived near trains more often than not even as an adult. Mom and Dad were both very active in the community: PTA, Girl Scouts, church leadership, and served as role models for me as I moved into the responsibilities of adulthood and into the field of social work, both as a therapist and community activist.

—Ginny, 50's

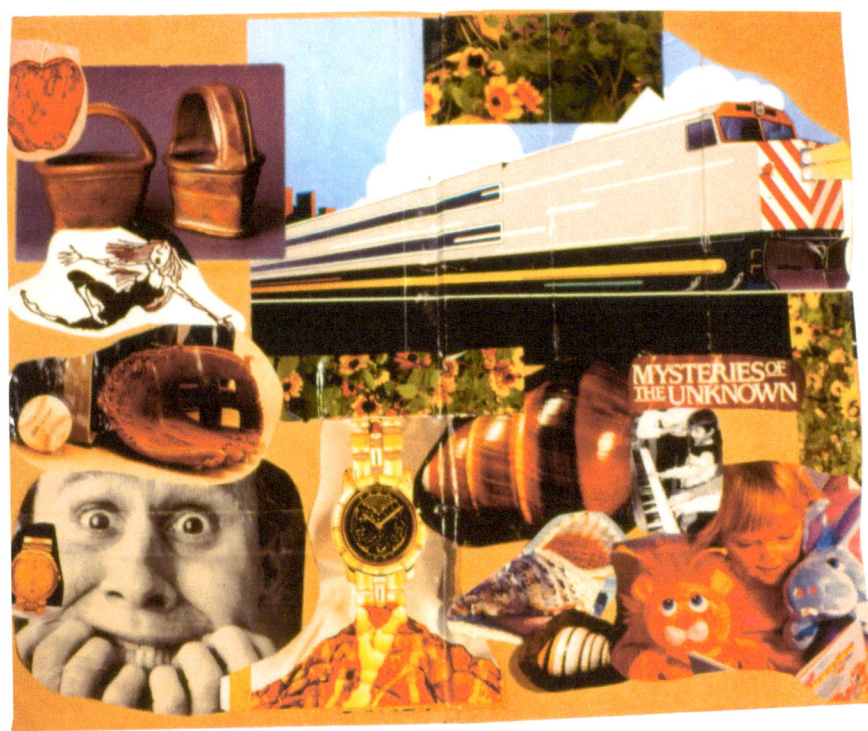

Train Speaks To Ginny:

I am sleek and get to where I'm going. I appreciate your heritage. You didn't get everything you needed, but you got enough and you can get for yourself what you need now. Stay on track and blow your horn when you need to. And don't let anyone stop you from getting to your destination!

Jo's Toy

I was asked to create an image exploring my favorite childhood toy. I chose to portray my piano, accompanied by my canary and my radio.

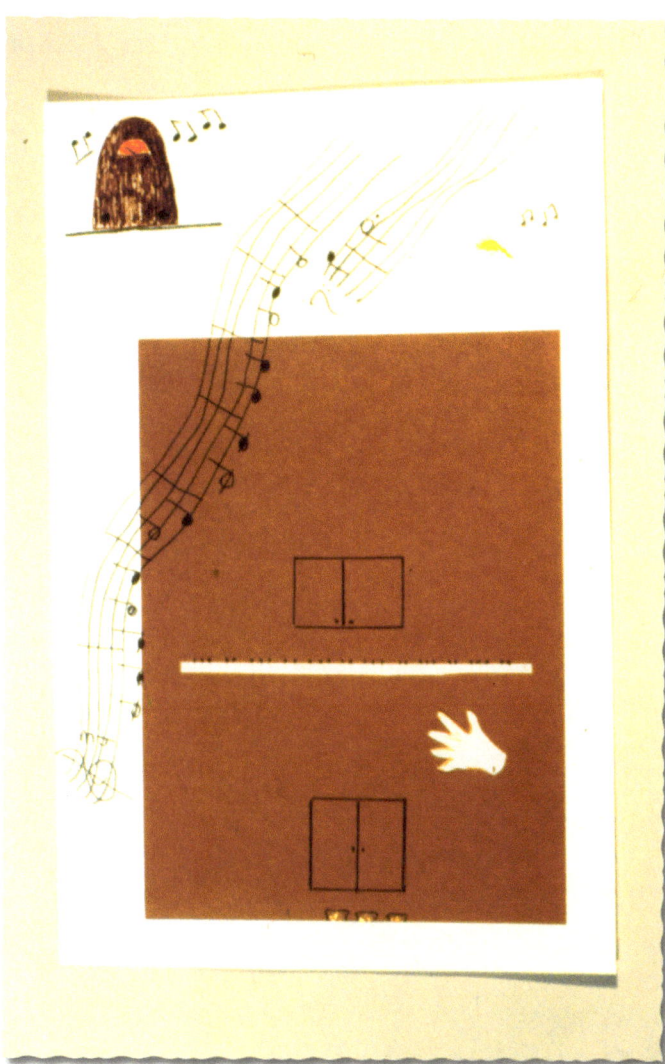

Piano Speaks To Jo:

Piano: *I'm the piano. I wish you didn't draw me so plain, but I know you loved me. We did exciting things. You did, with me. Do you miss me?*

Jo: *Sometimes, but I've forgotten that part.*

Piano: *But don't you remember how I could comfort you? You could use that.*

Jo: *I'm afraid. And I don't have time.*

Piano: *I gave you so much pleasure!!! Why are you afraid? It's your ears that are hungry. HA! And your eyes could use some exercise. Look at us.*

Jo: *I'm sorry. But your important parts show. I'm getting distracted. Are we through?*

Piano: *I'm more than just my important parts!*

Canary: *Don't you want to hear from me?*

Jo: *You weren't much of a pet for a four-year-old but M liked your singing so I did too.*

Canary: *It's not much of a life, locked in a cage. But thanks for playing the radio and the piano.*

Jo: *They comforted us both.*

Radio: *Yeah. I've been the one constant in your life. I gave you lots.*

Jo: *But you also waste some of my ear time. Audio junk food.*

When I made this collage, I explored the message in the last line of my dialogue with the radio, and became more conscious of my intake of "audio" junk food.

Almost two years later I reflected on my collage. I noticed the notion of "comfort" in much of my dialogue. I was surprised to realize that I received comfort from my radio, piano and canary. It sounds like I was a pretty sad little girl.

Music was important to me. Music was my home, somehow, but it was almost kept out of reach. I wanted to learn to play the piano before I was in kindergarten, but my mom wouldn't teach me until I could reach a full octave. So I pulled on my fingers!

Being allowed to practice would be like a privilege, something held out like a carrot. This kept me interested. I'm not sure whether my mom was clever or mean.

A Fine Golden Line

I completed this collage for an in-class assignment on "Play." After a meditation on childhood, the instructors suggested that participants play with the materials as if we were children.

The summer before this class, I traveled to Alaska for an extended family adventure. The trip turned out to be the high point of my life.

I have always thought that throughout life I had been spoiled with material goods and had never appreciated what I had. I had come to a point of adulthood asking myself, "Why do I feel so empty inside?"

The Alaska trip was my attempt to find a sense of fulfillment. "If this trip doesn't do it, nothing will," I said. Yet I wondered "Why go all the way to Alaska to find happiness?"

The collage is a rendition of my view from the ship of soft images of mountains, muted by the fog. The golden thread strings through the picture like an image of the fine golden line from Steppenwolf lyrics. I think of the gold thread in my collage as a life-line or path moving upward in a positive direction.

I had always assumed that my fulfillment would come with something really grand, something outside of myself, but in Alaska I learned that fulfillment comes from going within.

—Cheryl, 40's

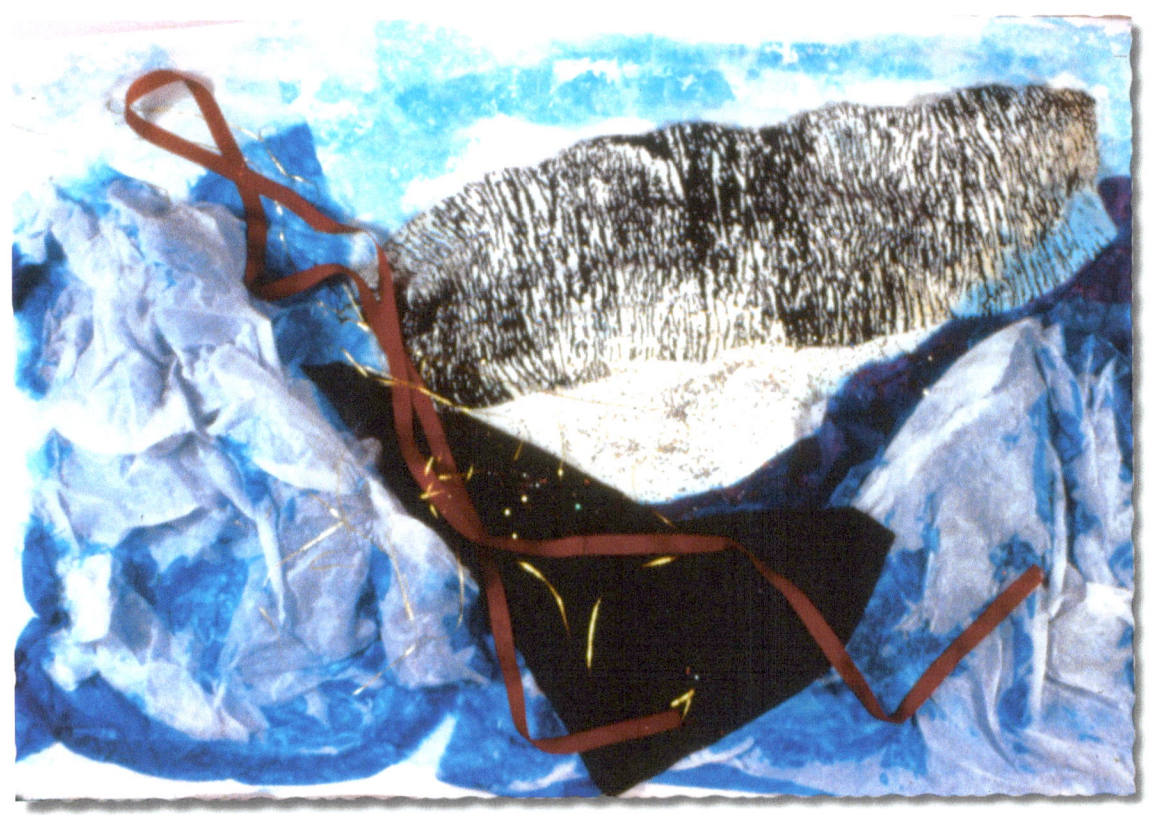

  Butterfly At Daybreak

CHAPTER FOUR

Expand And Deepen Your Self-Awareness

The Tree As Me

The creative urge lives and grows in the artist
like a tree in the earth from which it gets its nourishment.
We would as well, therefore, think of the creative process as a living thing,
implanted in the human psyche.

—C.G. Jung

The Tree As Me

This interesting experiment of designing yourself as a tree can be very informative. The roots, trunk, branches, leaves and other parts of the tree can represent different aspects of who you are. By doing this collage, you can develop a greater appreciation of your complexity and richness and gain a clearer awareness of your environment and your current needs. No need to have a particular issue for this collage.

Tree Questions To Ask Yourself

Imagine yourself as a tree and ask yourself these questions:

- What kind of tree would I be? Maple? Oak? Evergreen? Willow? etc.
- Am I small or tall? Am I a seedling, a mature tree, an ancient oak or perhaps a withering or a dying tree? Was I tended to as a young seedling or left to survive on my own?
- How deeply anchored is my root system?
- Is my bark thick and protective or thin and vulnerable? Has my bark been wounded? Has it healed?
- Is my trunk straight or crooked or a combination? Have I been battered or twisted by harsh weather or growing conditions?
- Do my branches need pruning to eliminate disease or to encourage new growth?
- Have I been cut back? Does this help me or hinder me?
- In what season do I find myself?
- Are there any other trees nearby?
- Am I similar to or different from the other trees?
- In what kind of environment do I find myself? The city? The seashore? Country? Desert?
- What weather surrounds me? Is there any water nearby?

- Do I have any animals around me or nesting in my branches? Am I overburdened by too many creatures living off of me?
- Am I surviving despite difficult circumstances?
- Notice other characteristics about your tree.
- What will I look like 10 years from now?

Constructing Your Tree

After giving some thought to these questions, choose magazine images and materials to construct your tree. (See Appendix B for ideas on materials.) You can also look for a picture of a tree in your magazines to use as the basis for your collage or try colored tissue paper and liquid laundry starch. They are fun to play with and easy to use.

Tissue Paper And Starch

Pieces of tissue can be torn by hand, placed on white paper and the starch applied over them with a brush. Different colors can be layered and pieces of tissue can be crinkled or wadded up to build up from the surface. When ready, brush starch over the tops of your raised areas to adhere the tissue to the surface. You needn't be neat in the use of these materials to produce a colorful, bold effect.

Remember, this is your make-believe tree; so use your imagination and create, create, create.

Getting To Know Your Tree

After completing your collage ask your tree to describe itself. We often find that our trees describe themselves in similar ways that we would describe ourselves. Sometimes our trees point out certain aspects of our lives which need attention or point out those good qualities and strengths that we are too modest to admit. Also ask your tree for words of wisdom or advice about a challenge in your life. This exercise is adapted from *Gardening in the Great Forest* by Doris Arrington.

(Review the section in Chapter 1, *Getting To Know Your Collage* and Chapter 2, *Conversing With Your Collage*.)

You can repeat this collage experience at monthly or yearly intervals to see how your tree might have changed.

Any object can be used as a metaphor for the self. What kind of forest, island, garden, animal or chair etc. would you be? This can be especially fun to explore in a group. What kind of animals would we be? Who would take which roles? If we were a garden, what kind would this group be? Which part of the garden would I represent?

There is only one journey. Going inside yourself.
—*Rainer Maria Rilke*

Wind And Tears

My tree is very much alive and full of wisdom, solid… reaching upward… unafraid to be open or exposed. I found the texture of the dried moss to be inviting. It asks to be touched. I joyfully sprinkled the leaves of paper confetti and sensed that motion was present in the art. All four seasons are represented in the tree. As the glue dripped, I envisioned the drip lines as "tears" which began to form the roots.

—Jo, 50's

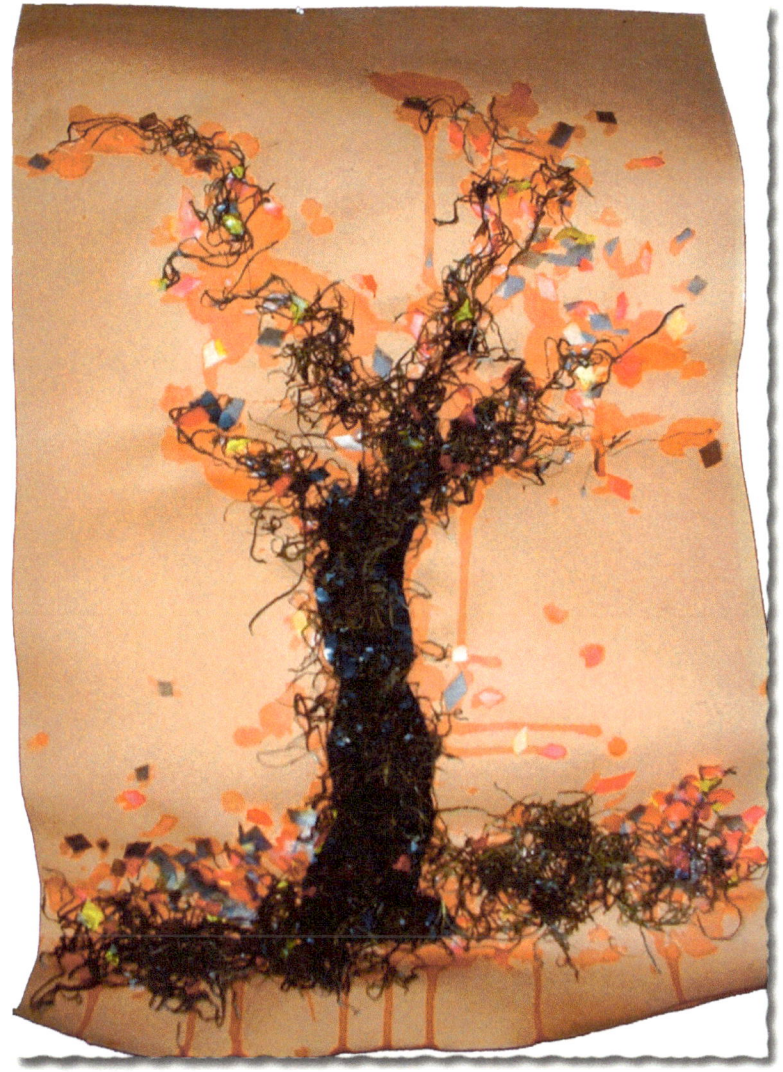

Tree Speaks To Jo:

Thank you for taking care of me, liking me,

I like tears.

I like my leaves floating in the art.

DO ART! Keep exploring. I like how I turned out, even though sometimes I don't make sense.

Wondering Tree

When I did this collage I had change in mind. I knew that changes were all around me and I was wondering what to do about them. I chose the image of the tree because it is a life-giving and growing image to me. It is always growing and reaching up. The roots are always growing deeper to stabilize no matter how big it gets.

The trunk of the tree holds the questions, Where is home? Where do I go? The word "wind" is how I feel; blown, carried by changes in the wind's path. There is a poem about things the wind does. As I write I realize that the changes/winds in my life are not bad, they seem to have no direction, but they are all there for some reason. And now looking at it I realize that I just have to trust that reason and let that be my roots. I need to sit back and enjoy the ride and the growth that is to come.

The top of the tree is sunlight shining through. It's really me looking to shed some light on these questions. The source of that light is in me.

On one side of the tree is a butterfly. To me it represents change and growth. It is me changing and growing and becoming what I can become. The butterfly told me not to get too comfortable in my cocoon. There are many great things awaiting me out there.

Then there is the moon; a crescent moon, not full. A symbol of women, feminine power. It controls the waves and cycles. It has much power in women's physical and emotional cycles. I wasn't sure why I put it there but now I see that it is the power I have inside of me that I want to reach.

This is a picture of my potential, what I have in me and what I need to find in me. The biggest challenge of this is to allow myself to be all these things. The tree is strong, letting the wind blow through me, rooted in the trust that the change will not blow me over.

The butterfly is beautiful and developed, able to soar on the wings I grew through challenges of the past.

The moon power that is in me, simple yet so powerful, leads me to the source of my strength.

I am Woman.

—Lisa, 20's

Lisa's Butterfly Speaks:

I am your butterfly. I feel peace and let my wings rely on the wind. Many changes have shaped me. Lisa, do not let the cocoon become too comfortable. There are many wonders awaiting you outside.

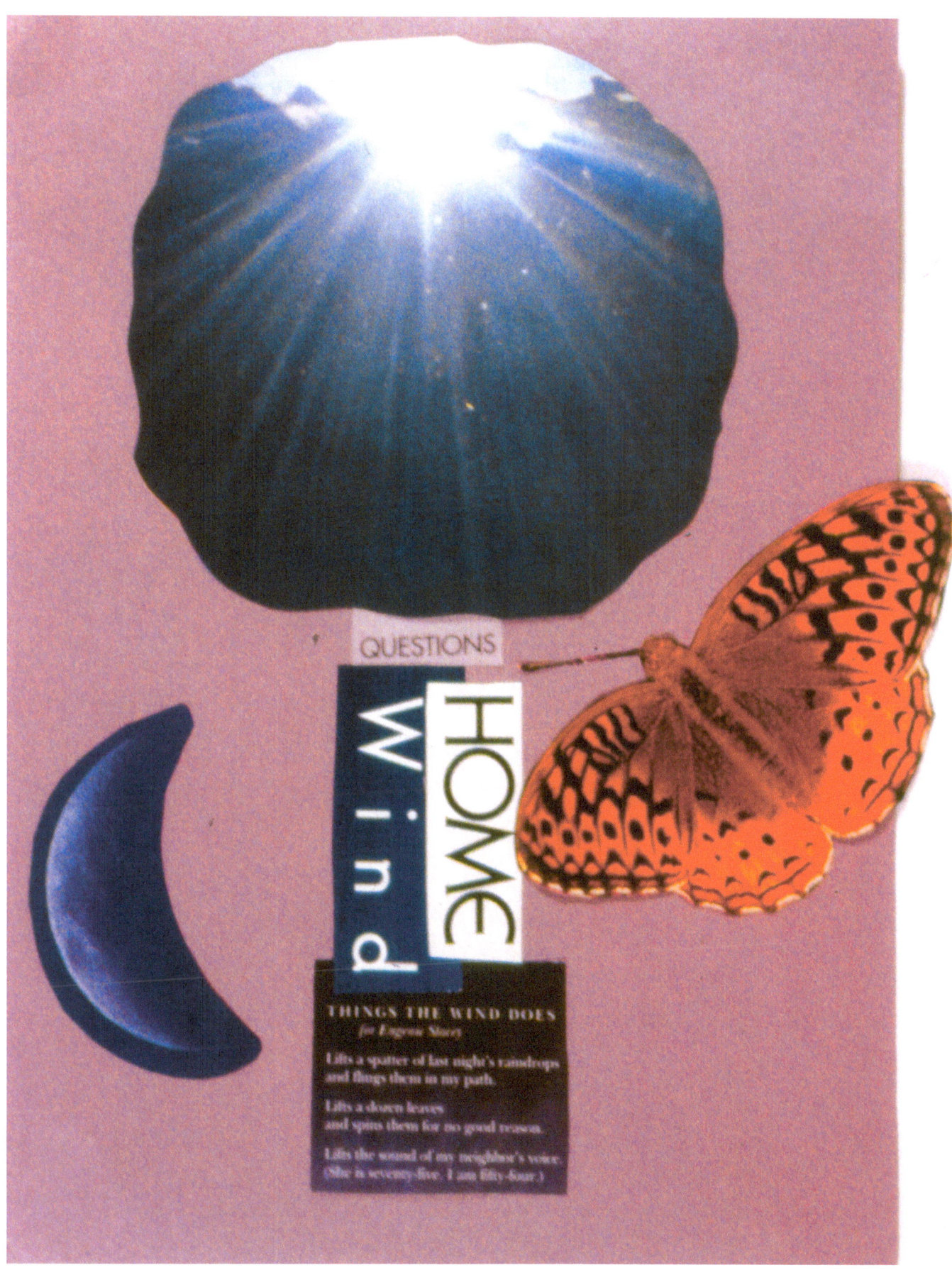

QUESTIONS

Wind

HOME

THINGS THE WIND DOES
for Eugene Shore

Lifts a spatter of last night's raindrops
and flings them in my path.

Lifts a dozen leaves
and spins them for no good reason.

Lifts the sound of my neighbor's voice.
(She is seventy-five. I am fifty-four.)

From Seedling To Snag

Only a few feathers covered my tree at first. Several weeks later I realized that I'm really in the autumn of my life. The stars, sun and moon which I was reaching for earlier in my life, building a family and a career, are no longer my focus. So I added a lot more feathers to the tree branches. The stars, sun and moon are now hidden from view by the leaves. Now I appreciate all the discoveries which bring me wisdom as I grow older. The angels, key and unlocked heart remind me that I can go straight to the Source – to God – for help. The affirmations, written on paper, each tell their own chapter in my life story. "Reconciliation" and "Holiness" are hidden in the tree.

—Sharon, 50's

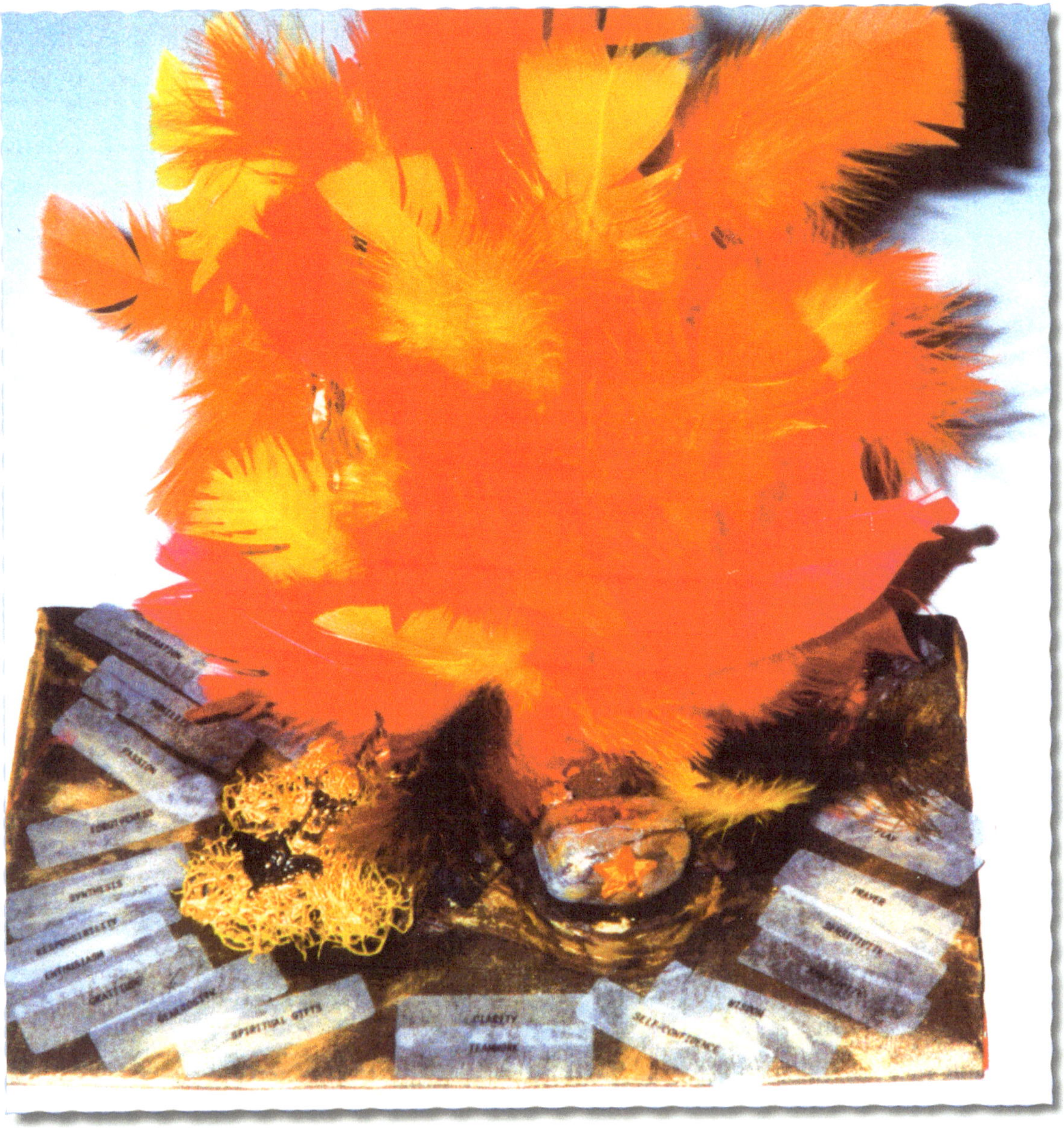

Butterfly At Daybreak

Solid As A Rock

The mirror "knothole" lets me see myself when I look at my tree. I was surprised to hear my tree say that it is rooted in New England. My parents grew up there and I was conceived there, but I grew up in Illinois.

Apparently, my first "roots" are really in New England!

—Ginny, 50's

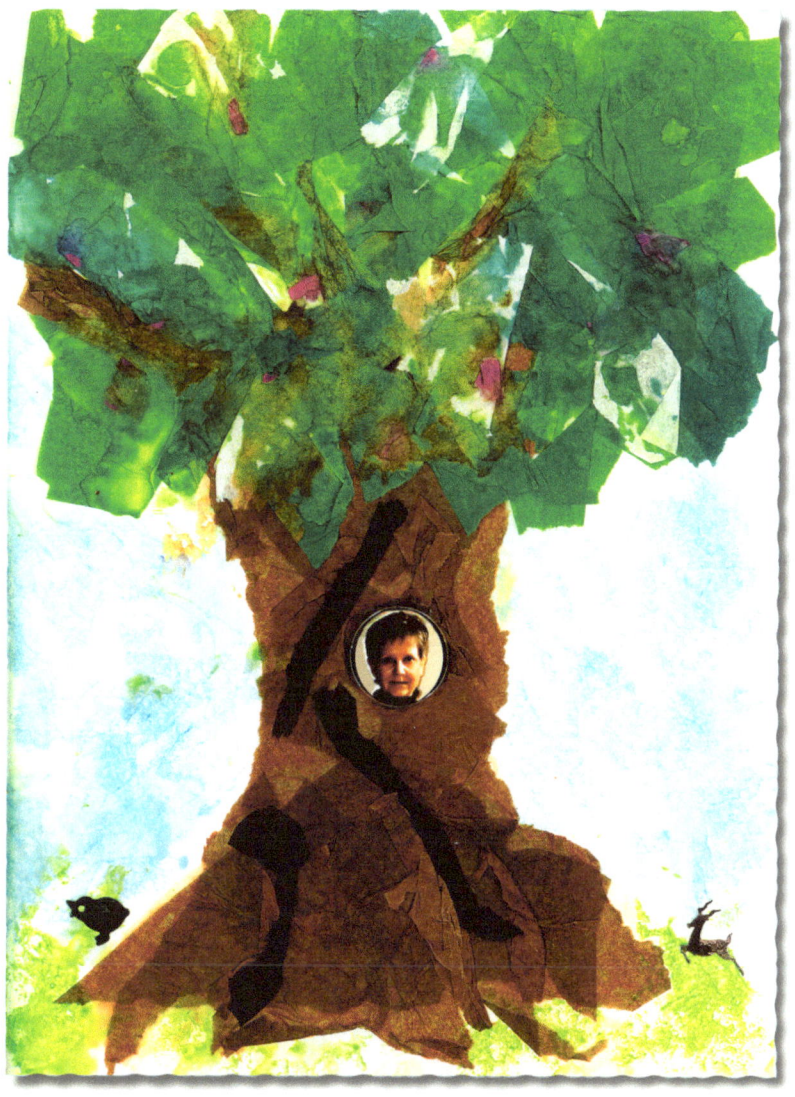

Tree Speaks To Ginny:

I'm here to stay, solid as a rock, and my roots are probably wrapped around some rocks in this New England soil, impervious to the hurricanes! Just try me! In me, you see all of your power, beauty and color. Shake your leaves a bit – let your hair down. Celebrate the moments of life. There are no unimportant moments. I don't let small thoughts or doubts contain me. I'm blooming even in my maturity.

Grieving Tree

I created this page in my collage journal after my
father died.

—Ginny, 50's

where many have gone before. I am not alone, crazy, or having a nervous breakdown. My heart is at work, my soul is awake. Mary M. Funk.

When tears come, I breathe deeply and rest. I know I am swimming in a hallowed stream

I am timeless

It's OK to cry

CHAPTER FIVE

Transitions In Our Lives: Bridges To The Unknown

You have to leave the city of your comfort
to go into the wilderness of your intuition.
What you discover will be wonderful,
What you'll discover will be yourself.

—*Alan Alda*

Transitions

We inevitably make transitions in our lives. We are always in the process of change. These passages can be rich with opportunities to deepen life experience and increase resiliency. Nevertheless, they are often accompanied by regrets and fears of the unknown.

Many transitions occur naturally as we develop and evolve from birth to old age. There are planned transitions which can be anticipated with excitement and joy. Other changes are unwelcome and unexpected. At times we are sad about leaving situations and people behind, sometimes with much left unsaid. Transitions in our lives can occur with regard to friends and family, partners, career, education, children, health and geographical location.

With every movement forward we are leaving something behind. Can we let go of it? Can we grieve the loss and move ahead?

Bridges

A bridge connects the place where you've been to the place that you are going. This collage will help you take a look at where you are now, where you want to go, and how far you've come.

What Kind of Bridge Would I Be?

Before you begin your work, make the journey to the present moment. Relax, focus on your breath and let go of thoughts of the day that wander in and out of your consciousness.

Pretend that you are a bridge and ask yourself "What kind of a bridge would I be?" Bridges come in all shapes and sizes from the Golden Gate to a small plank of wood over a little creek. Imagine what your bridge would look like. Next, think of a scene or image that represents your present life or recent past that you are leaving behind and imagine that image on the left side of your bridge. On the other side of the bridge imagine an image or scene of your future that you are moving toward. Is there something you could bring with you to help you on your way?

Create your bridge and your scenes of the past and future using an image of a bridge or any craft materials you would like. When your collage is completed, converse with your bridge and any of your images. *(Refer to Chapter 2)* Let the bridge describe itself and ask it for information that will be helpful to you in your transition.

Getting To Know Your Bridge

- What kind of a bridge are you?
- Where are you on that bridge?
- Does the description of your bridge speak to the way in which you would describe yourself or would like to be described?
- Is there more detail ahead in the future or behind in the past?
- Which part of the collage draws you toward it?
- Which part repels?
- What have you learned from your bridge?
- What feelings are you feeling right now?
- What other questions do you need to ask in order to fully understand this collage?
- What images or objects can you take from your past with you over the bridge to help you in the future?
- What would you title your collage?

Remember. Simply making this collage will be creative, informative, and worthy. Conversing with the images, asking questions of them, will take you further if this interests you at this moment.

"What if imagination and art are not frosting at all,
  but the fountainhead of human experience?"
                                              —*Rollo May*

"They must often change who would be
   constant in happiness or wisdom."
                                              —*Confucius*

Walking Ahead With Confidence

I have many good memories of my visits to Cape Cod. When I saw this image of a beach boardwalk, I knew it was right for my bridge.

The images at the bottom represent my past. My experience of childhood and young adulthood was one of being out of touch with my feelings, particularly anger and sadness. Looking back on it, my feelings were very much frozen and I felt tight and contained and out of touch with my body. I remember being aware of time but was always focused on the future when I would finally achieve my goals, never seeming to be feeling free in the present moment.

As I entered my 30's, I began to feel myself "thawing out" and loosening up, both my body and my emotions. I began to blossom and bloom, finding previously unexpressed feelings and playful parts of my personality. The images at the topside of the bridge represent my life at present and form a vision for my future. I find more color in my life and the earth is my "palette."

I do have a sense that my path in life is returning me to the potential "full self" to which I was actually born.

—Ginny, 50's

Bridge Speaks To Ginny:

I'M YOUR BRIDGE. I connect you with your dreams. I am simply built of natural products and I age gradually. I look more and more beautiful with the passage of time. My railings protect you from falling. My planks are aligned in good order. I am sunk solidly into the ground. I am recyclable! From nature I come, to nature I return. Walk ahead with confidence. You have all that you need.

Looking back on this collage five years later, I'm still amazed at how far I've come. The "future" illustrated in my collage has become the "present," and I'm mostly delighted about where I am now despite the continued challenges of my life.

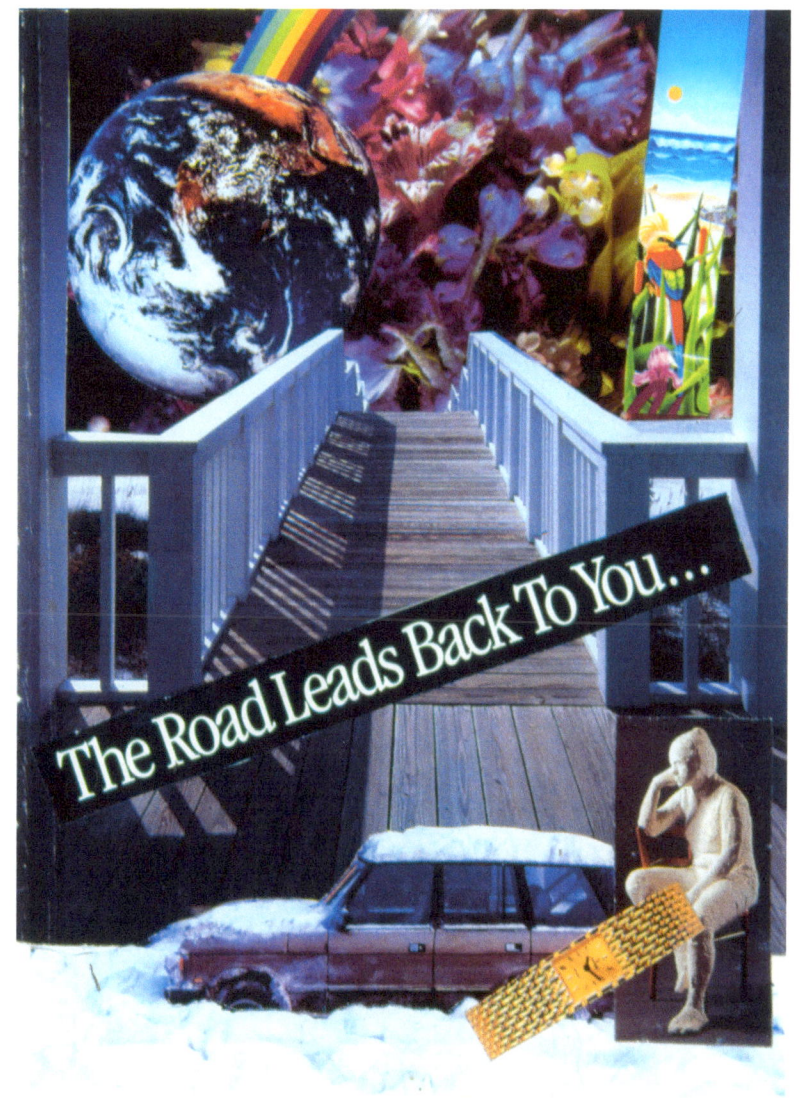

The Road Leads Back To You...

Tied In Knots

I spent the class hour just involved in tying all the knots. It proved to be a very frustrating experience, tangled, confused, uneven.

Later, I realized I had included 17 planks, so each one represents a year of my life.

—Laura, teens

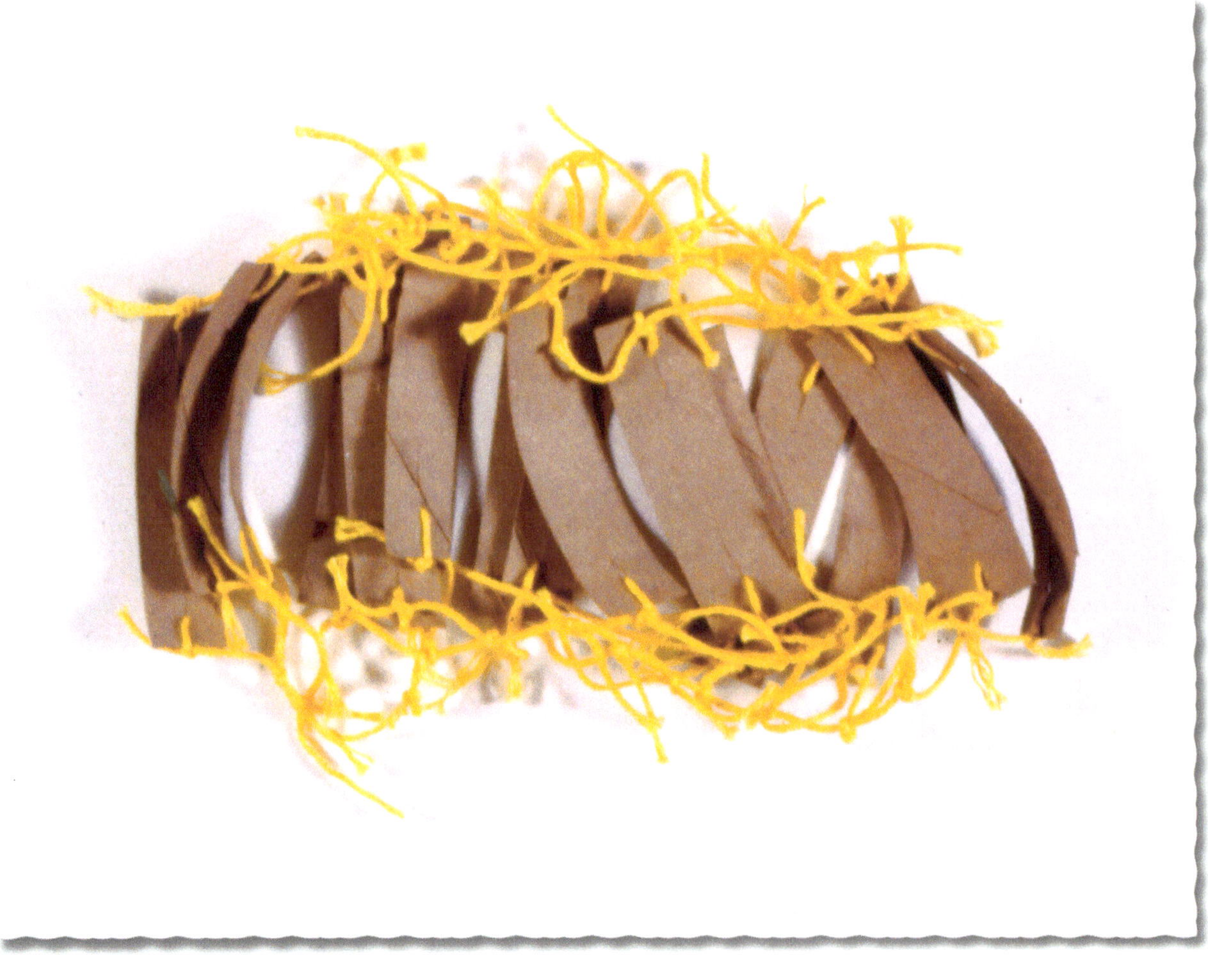

Bridge Speaks To Laura:

Warning, proceed with caution, watch your step!

Laura Speaks To Bridge:

It would be scary to cross you. However, it is the only way to get to the other side.

Lost And Found

My bridge piece was a bit difficult for me to do. I knew exactly what symbol I wanted to use for my bridge but I did not know how to illustrate it and not be threatening to the rest of the class. I guess I was really just a little scared that people would judge or not like me if I started to talk about religion. It was hard for me to make the cross. I knew I wanted it to glow so I used the gold and the silver glitter, but it would not dry. Every time I picked up the paper the glue would run and get all clumpy. It finally started to dry but the glue dried sloppy and outside the lines. I decided to cut it and paste it on another paper but the glue was not totally dried and that was another problem in itself. When the words "lost" and "found" came to me I started to perk up. I then conversed with my bridge. I was so happy with my conversation that I decided to put it right on the collage. Right then I knew that it was complete. I received some really great feedback from class members especially on the cross. I was happy with my project and with myself, even if my cross was not exactly how I wanted it. That was a BIG step for me!!!!!

—Stacie, 20's

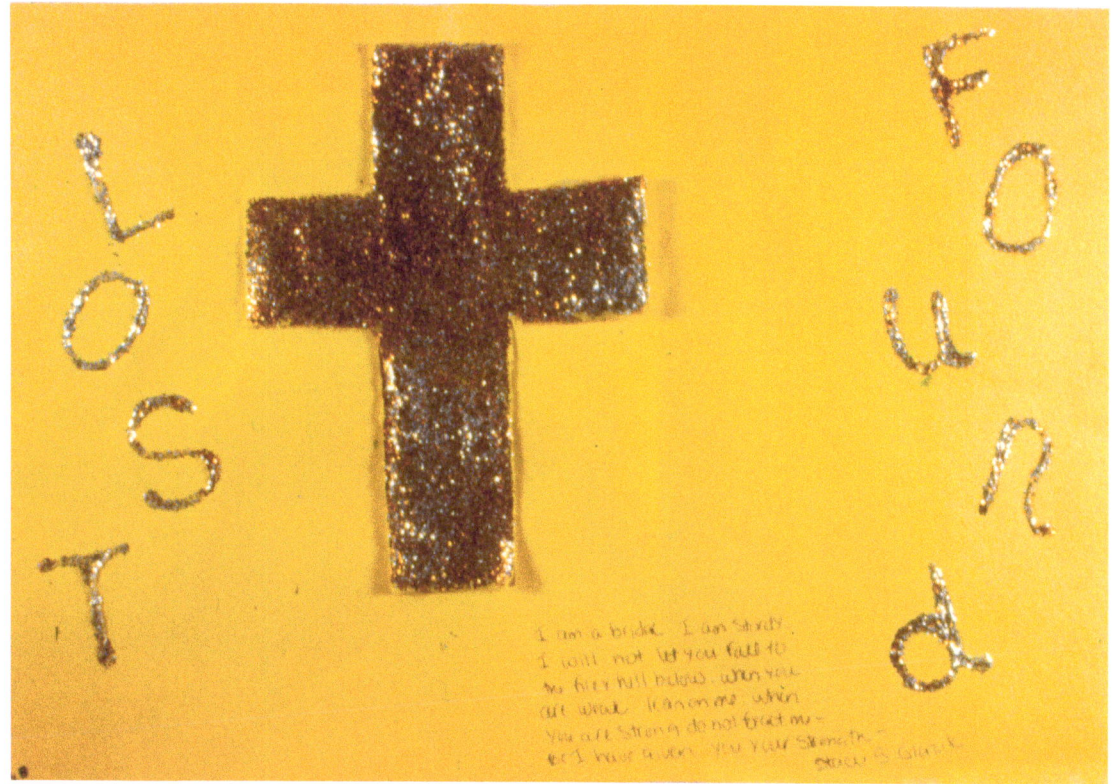

Bridge Speaks To Stacie:

I am a bridge. I am sturdy. I will not let you fall to the fiery hell below. When you are weak, lean on me. When you are strong, do not forget me for I have given you strength.

A Small Stream Easily Crossed

When I began putting this together I realized that I had many unhappy and unresolved feelings about my life. Putting them down in a concrete form was unsettling.

On a board much like a game board is the story of my life. About two-thirds of this board is green to depict life and growth. A blue stream crosses the board. On the other side purple represents over 50 years old. The black square with the skeleton represents death. At one corner of the green portion is a yellow rectangle with a picture of a baby on it. This is me at birth. From that square marching in the direction of the bridge are the following representations of me as stand-up figures. As a young girl, as a teenager/young adult joyfully riding the back of my boyfriend/husband, as a pregnant woman, as a mother with two young sons and as a supermom. The last image is on the bridge.

On the far side of the bridge are three female friends with their arms around each other. They are marching off to the future together. The bridge represents where I am now in my life and the three women represent me and two good friends who support one another through the difficulties of the sandwich generation: kids to complete raising and parents to be taking ever more responsibility for. Beyond the three women, continuing toward the far corner are the three women now older. Beyond them on the purple, ever closer to the final corner are two even older women. The third has died. Finally at the right, front corner is a picture of a skeleton, flat, for that is where I will be one day, lying in the earth. Above the skeleton is a picture (my picture) in an oval frame. This is the last tangible reminder of my life.

—Marcia, 40's

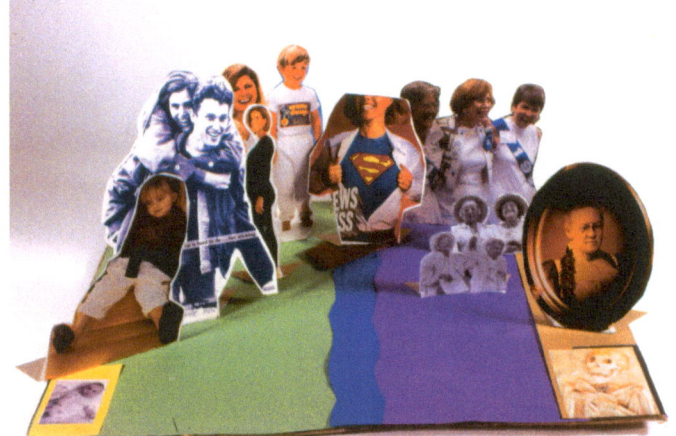

Marcia Converses With Bridge:

Marcia: *Why are you such a short little span, not more than a couple of tree trunks thrown together over a stream?*

Bridge: *Were you expecting something grander, more like the Golden Gate Bridge or that hideously high, narrow one you had to drive over in Vancouver?*

Marcia: *Ah, grand and high are not necessary here. Much better to view one's midlife transition as a small stream to be crossed easily rather than a raging torrent fraught with danger.*

Bridge: *Exactly, just a small step up. My boards are broad and sturdy. You can count on me to support you while you cross.*

Marcia: *What reassurance. It's wonderful to know that I can count on you while going through a change.*

Bridge: *I am here for you.*

Reaching Out

My bridge between my past and the present is represented by a hand. The only things I depicted from my past are the people with whom I keep in contact. These are the beans. Everything I didn't want to keep slipped through the fingers. There are many things about my past that I'd like to forget and let go of. The stronger I get, the further behind the darkness is.

—Lisa, 20's

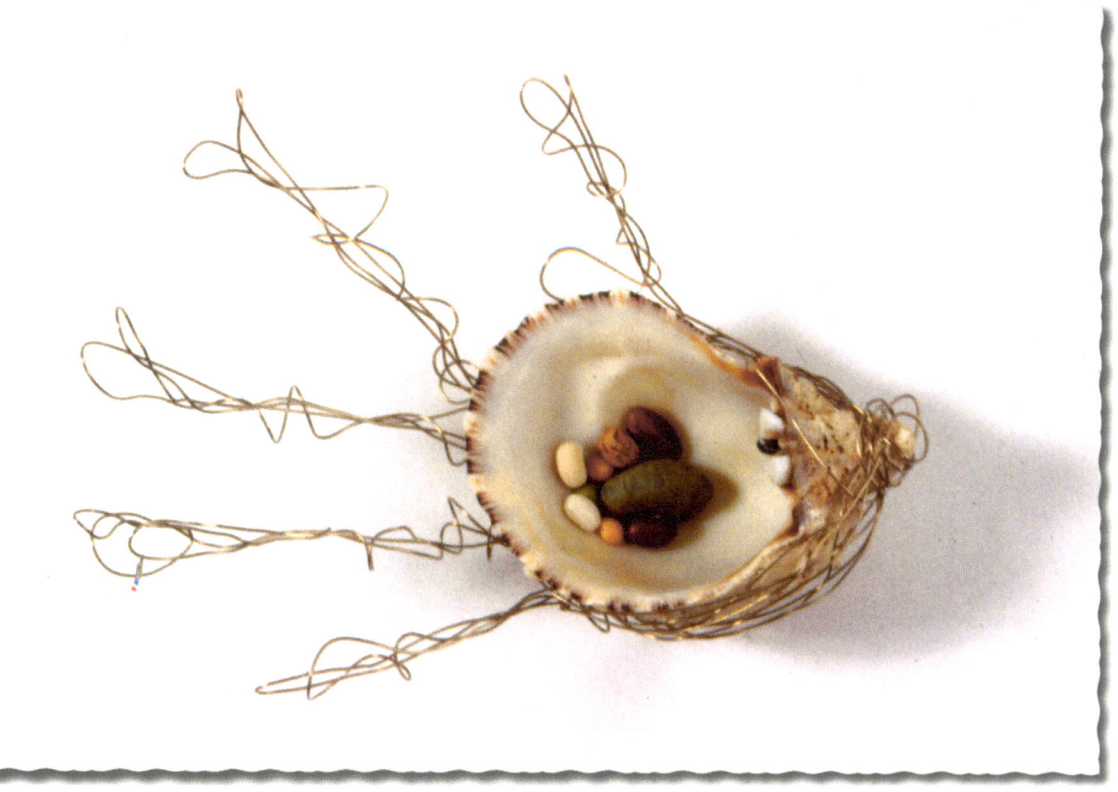

Hand Speaks To Lisa:

My fingers filter the good from the bad. I am a connection, reaching out to grasp the future. I am holding on to the past. I need to remain stable.

I will help you grasp the present if you trust me. I will never let go of anything you need but will keep it safely in my hand. I am open to what's ahead. Remember the tokens of the past and use that knowledge for the future. Each day a gem rolls through. Pay attention to the present. I hold no regrets.

I am obviously still struggling with some guilt and pain from last year. I need to move forward. The hand inside me has told me that it is okay. The things I have let go of are the dependency on drugs. Okay, so I need to work a little harder sometimes. Second guessing myself can still be a problem but I've come a long way! The dependence on myself and God is what is very important to me right now. Learning to trust what he tells me and not to be afraid to act on it. I have been given a lot of power inside. It feels good to say that. I have power and I know what I feel.

There's Always A Way To Cross The River

Tall bridges used to scare me when I was a child growing up near St. Louis. But when I chose a picture of a bridge to represent my move from Chicago to rural Iowa, I wanted a strong, tall bridge to help me through this major transition.

I was anxious about this move, but my husband and I were both feeling overwhelmed by the crowds and the traffic of the metropolitan area and yearned for a quieter, greener environment. We're living now in a small town with a very active arts, educational and environmentally-conscious population and we are happy to be here.

—Ginny, 50's

Bridge Speaks To Ginny:

Your life may feel like this now, swaying back and forth from side to side, blown by the breeze, never quite sure when you will find the next turn in the road. Leaving Chicago for Iowa has taken courage, but by now, you know you are in the right place. Looking back over your shoulder, you can no longer see Chicago (nor do you want to) but you have warm and wonderful memories of friends left behind, friends who share your love of creating collage and sharing the resultant bold images, insights, tears and laughter. Their energy will always be there for you, as will yours for them. In some respects, you are still arriving in Iowa, still finding ways to solidly plant your feet on this side of the bridge. Don't worry. There are people waiting for you, though they don't all know it yet. You will meet each other, other harmonious souls, and you will walk together on this side of the bridge. Know that there is always a way to cross the river, no matter how deep or swift the water.

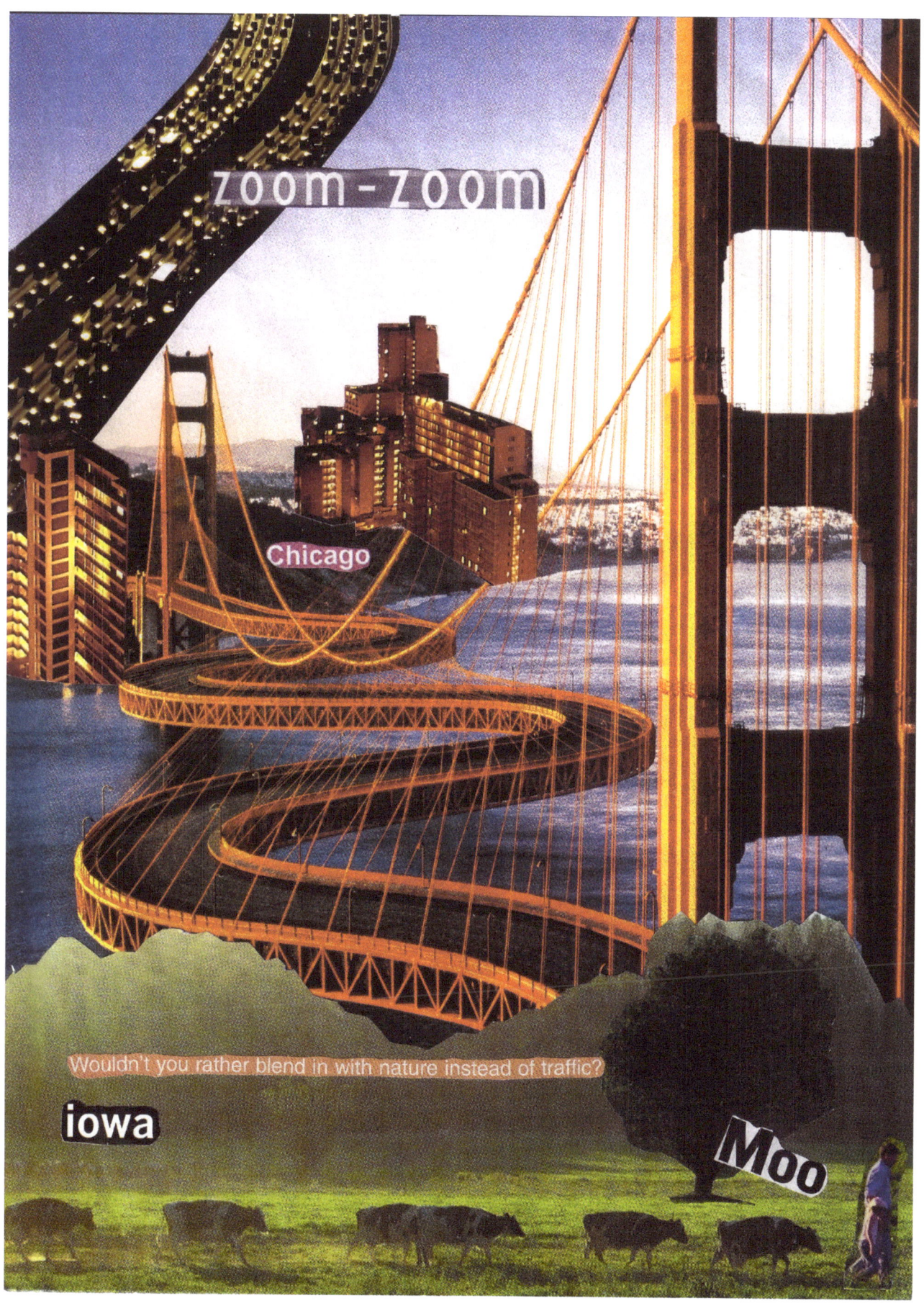

Filling The Inside Of My Soul

My bridge is three-dimensional; a covered bridge under the snow-covered winter trees, with a blazing fire burning inside.

—Amanda, 20's

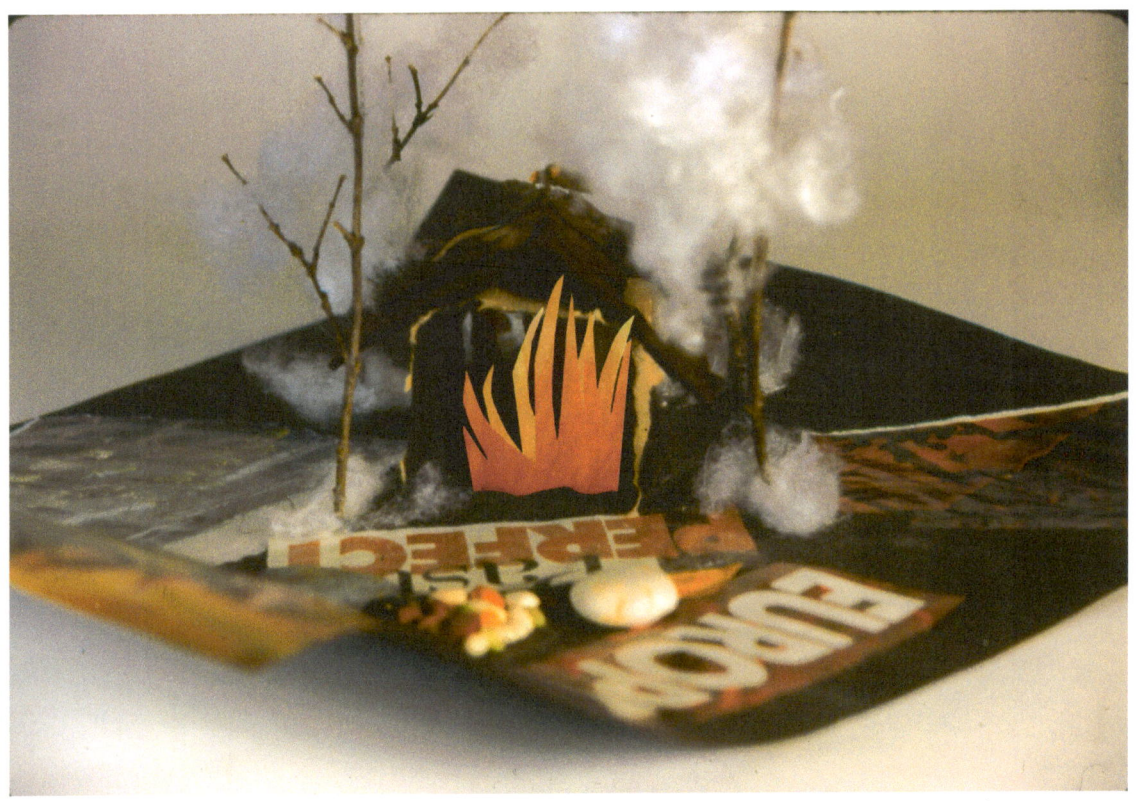

Covered Bridge Speaks To Amanda:

Amanda, you were blind. You thought that this life had a safe path for your heart and your soul but as in love, you could not see for yourself. As hollow as you were, there was an aware soul. Now you are filling the inside. There are bridges ahead. It is hard to comprehend but they quite possibly are more tortuous than this. There are many more experiences ahead in life for you. And, again, you will be blind and less of a strong person before you cross, but this lifetime, however long, will prove you true! There may be blood on your hands. Be brave, be strong, and be true. In hope...

CHAPTER SIX

Once Upon A Time

Fairy Tales, Stories, And Favorite Childhood Songs Revisited

It is yourself that must constantly be transforming.
You cannot bring the same stale self to the world
and expect the world to be new for you.

—Deepak Chopra

Fairy tales, childhood stories, and songs bring back many childhood memories. These memories are a unique lens through which we see how our lives have changed since childhood. With this new awareness and insight you will see options and choices you might never have noticed before.

Your First Interpretation

To begin, choose a favorite fairy tale or childhood story or song and allow yourself some time to review the story or song in your mind. Go back over the words and visualize the images in your mind's eye. Illustrate a part or all of the tale or song using whatever materials you wish. After making your collage, take some notes or think about how the story, lyrics, or characters were similar to your childhood experience and the people in your life. Talk with your images and ask for clarification about any childhood issues which still concern you. (See Chapter 1: Getting To Know Your Collage and Chapter 2: Conversing With Your Collage.)

Changing Interpretation

Let some time go by, a week or more, and then change your original collage in some way to show how life has changed since childhood and what your life is like now. Some possibilities include adding images or materials to your original collage or taking your original collage apart and reassembling all the pieces in a new way. Maybe you'll want to take your original collage apart and use some of the images and materials as the basis for a new collage. After making your changes, take a few moments to converse with your new collage. Ask your collage images for wisdom and insight about current challenges or questions. What do these changes tell you about yourself?

"It is above all by the imagination that
we achieve perception and compassion and hope."

—Ursula K. Le Guin

Wish You Were Here

Part 1

As I was doing this collage I was happy. This collage is about a song that my father would sing to us, and I was singing it all the while I worked. The song goes:

The man in the moon who sailed the sky was the most courageous skipper, but he made a mistake when he tried to take a drink of milk from the dipper. He dipped it into the Milky Way, he carefully, cautiously filled it, but when the little bear howled and the big bear growled, it frightened him so that he spilled....Tickle, tickle....

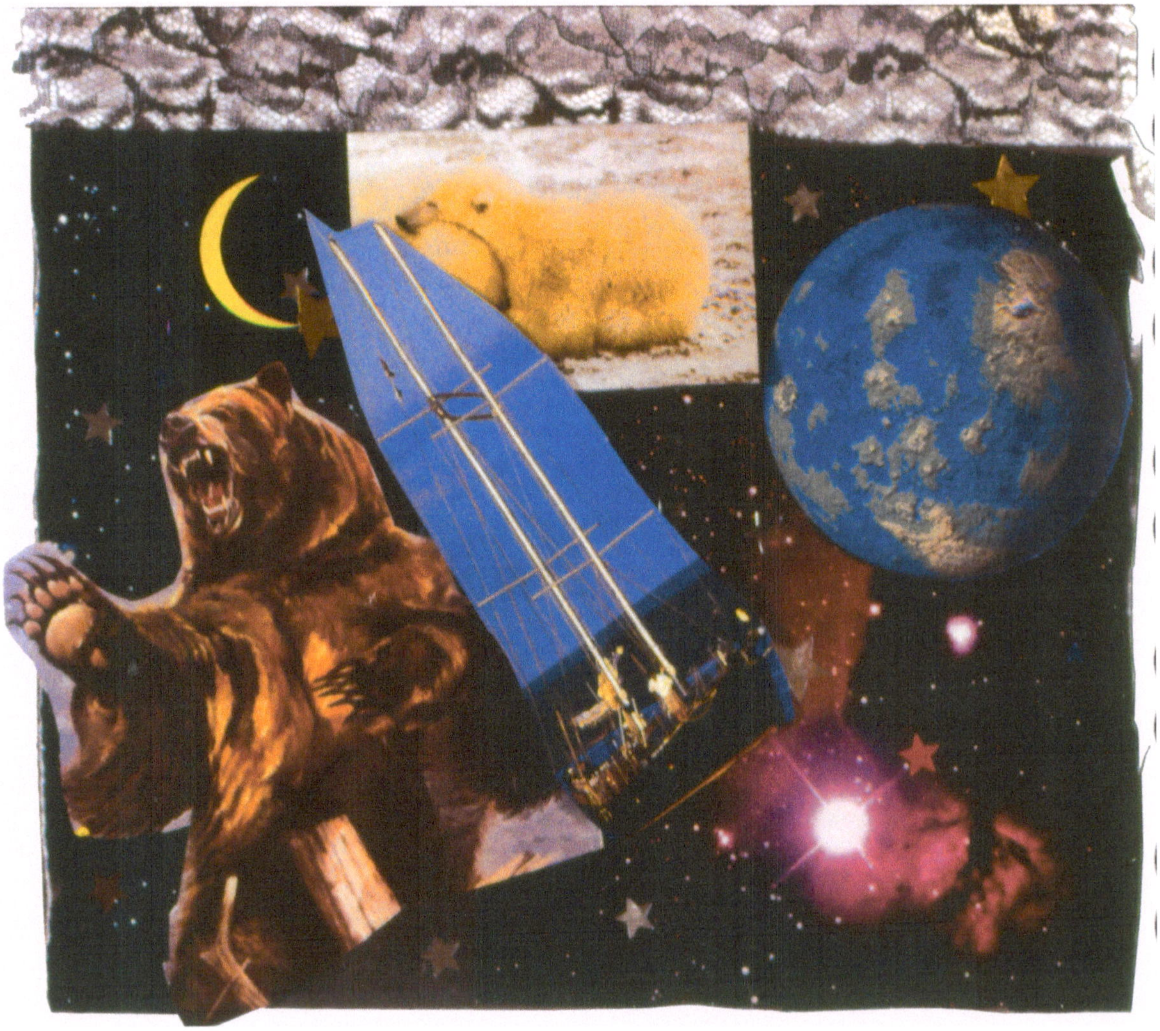

    Butterfly At Daybreak

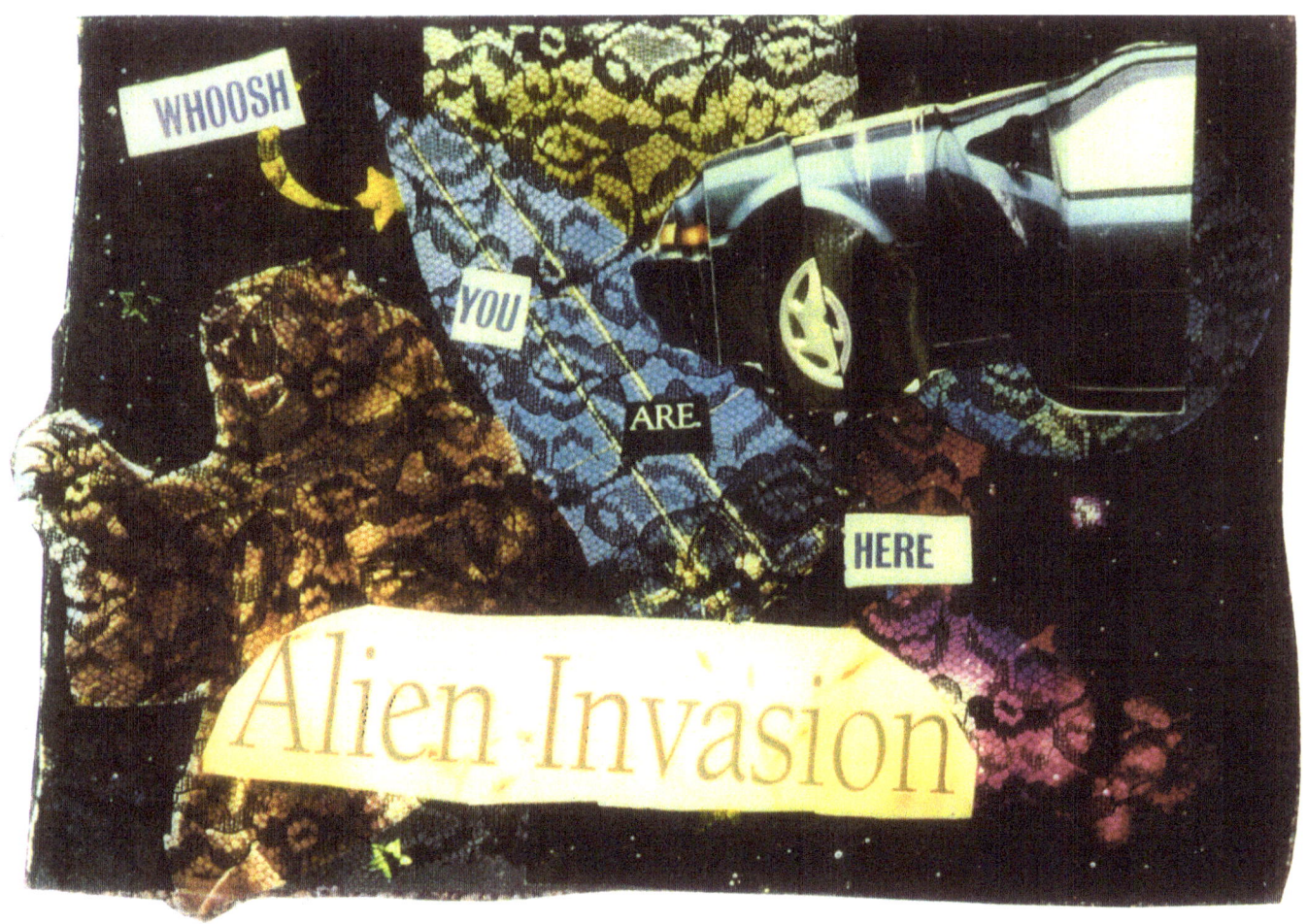

Part 2

I was not happy about changing this collage, not because I would have to destroy my original piece, but because my life changed in some very sad ways.

When I was about 6 years old, my father was in a terrible car accident, and although he lived he was not the same. I do not remember a lot of how it was but my mother and my older sisters do. They have told me that our father was the type of man that loved to come home from work and have his kids greet him at the door, asking each one of us how the day went and kissing and hugging us as he made his way to our mother.

After the accident, he became a stranger even to my mother. He did not play with us as much, he would yell at us for making too much noise when he came home from work and he would rather have us play outside until dinner. I put a black veil over the top of my original collage with a crunched car and the words "Whoosh you are here … Alien invasion" to represent how fast this story changed. I titled it Wish You Were Here.

—Karen, 30's

Little House In The Big Woods

I have early memories of reading, reading, reading, finishing all of my books in the car on the way home from the library! The favorite ones stand out: The story of a pioneer family, close-knit, struggling to survive, happy in hardship, because of family strength, spirit and innate goodness. I returned as an adult, to the birthplace of the story. The mighty big woods are long gone, but the beauty and the true spirit of the family remains.

I have a photo of the spot where their log cabin stood. The expansive sunset spreads above this place of humble beginnings, the imaginary companions of my childhood. I am inspired by the example of strength and perseverance of this line of women; the trail blazers, the survivors, the storytellers who inspire me with courage.

I look for pictures to help me and the story begins to unfold; not my story but the story of the pioneer woman who told her story. As I made my collage, I realized that as I age, I am seeking the story of my own ancestors, the story I will never know; a lost story of persecution, escape, travel to new land and endless struggle. I seek to imagine the story of my beginnings. I seek to tell their story through my art, to give my people a remembrance, to leave their names alive for the future. I seek to keep them alive and known and powerful.

—Gerri, 50's

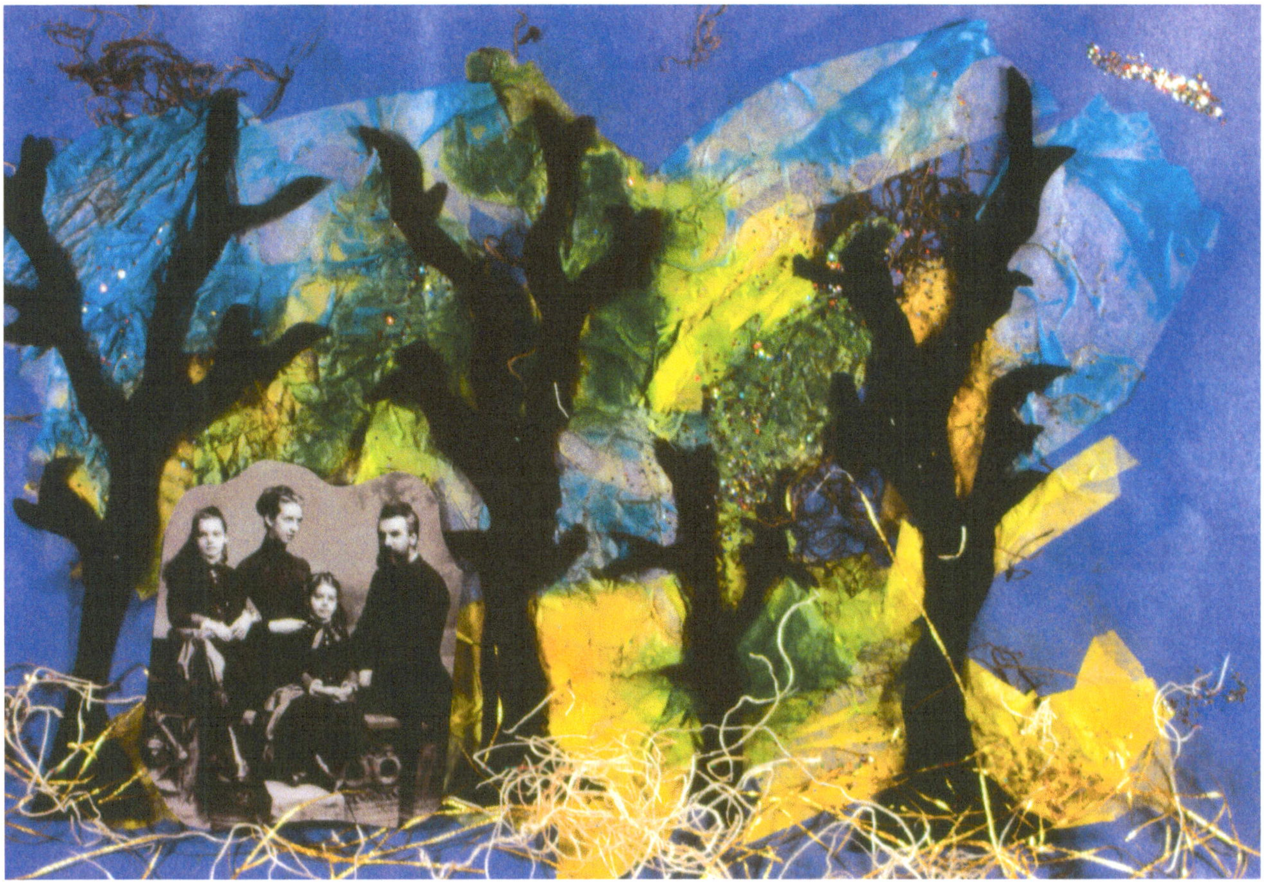

Where's My Prince?

I knew Cinderella was a favorite childhood fairy tale but hadn't understood why. I dissected my reasons. As I prepared to do my collage, I let myself feel the emotions evoked as I remembered the elements of the story from beginning to end. Then I looked for magazine pictures, etc. that expressed those feelings. (Part II shown here).

Transforming this piece to a more current "fit," I cut away the despair and downtrodden section and accordion-pleated it to signify the up-and-down, transitory nature of feelings.

Another significant change was taking the original "man-rescuing woman" section and cutting and rearranging. Each person now stood side-by-side, she wearing less fluff and he with a larger head.

How good it once felt to be rescued. How I waited for that to happen in my life. Where is my prince? Yet the prince was never good enough and the despair never went away. I would wait for the next prince to come.

This collage helped me recognize my past need to be rescued and the independence I now feel.

—Susan, 50's

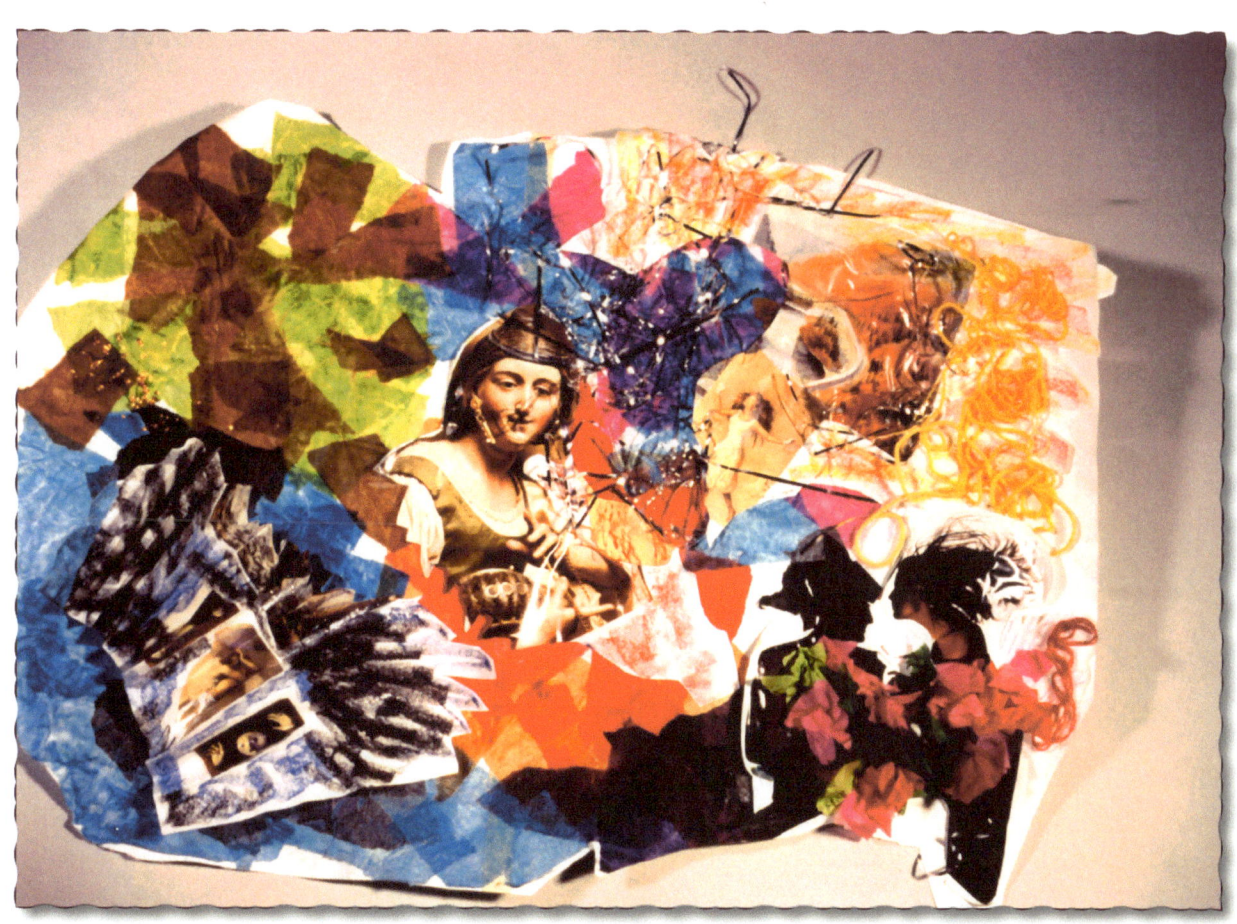

Hansel And Gretel

I started with a vivid idea: the depiction of the Hansel and Gretel fairy tale. The 19th Century engraving of the two young girls collecting greens in the forest seemed perfect to represent the children. Now the witch. She needed to be in the oven; the victorious triumph of the bright children over the cruel and wily adult. Unfortunately, no black-hatted crones with a warty nose and a broom stick presented themselves. In desperation I flipped through a copy of "Martha Stewart Living" and then it hit me! This woman, Martha Stewart, despite an attractive outward appearance, was just as wily about getting me to bake gourmet fantasies in my own oven as the old crone was about getting the children into her oven! I had my witch. Adding the tissue paper flames of red, orange and yellow was immensely satisfying. I was laughing aloud with pleasure. I was the innocent child roasting my nemesis!

—Marcia, 40's, (created 1997)

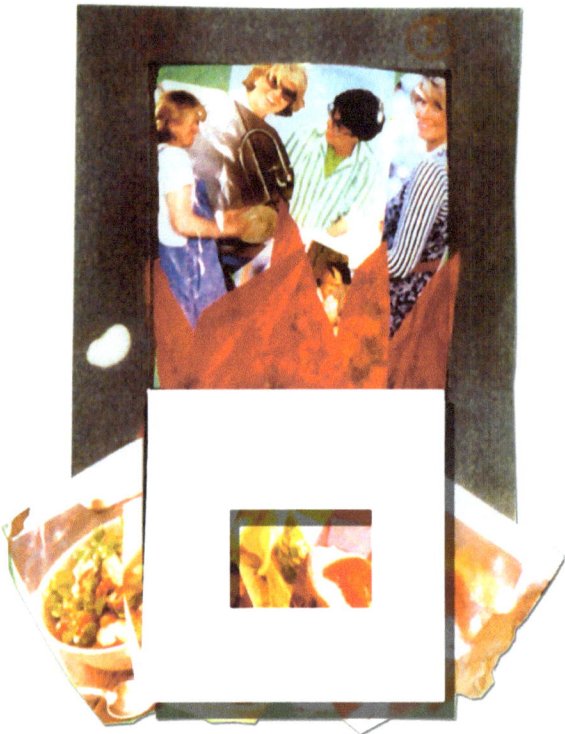

Part 1: Marcia Speaks With Martha Stewart:

Martha Stewart: *What is it about my wonderful self which causes you to view me as the wicked witch of the hearth, home and garden? I am here to help you to live more beautifully; to create lovely surroundings and delicious food.*

Marcia: *How presumptuous of you! How dare you have the gall to tell me or anyone else for that matter that you know answers for our everyday happiness. You are just projecting on to everyone else your particular extraordinary fantasy of what a princess's castle should look like and how a princess should act and be like. You may have a staff of 150 to create this unrealistic expectation of life in the U.S. in the 1990s (the princess always has maids, etc.), but the rest of us DON'T! You make us unhappy and dissatisfied if we don't live up to your standards! Always striving, never quite achieving it all.*

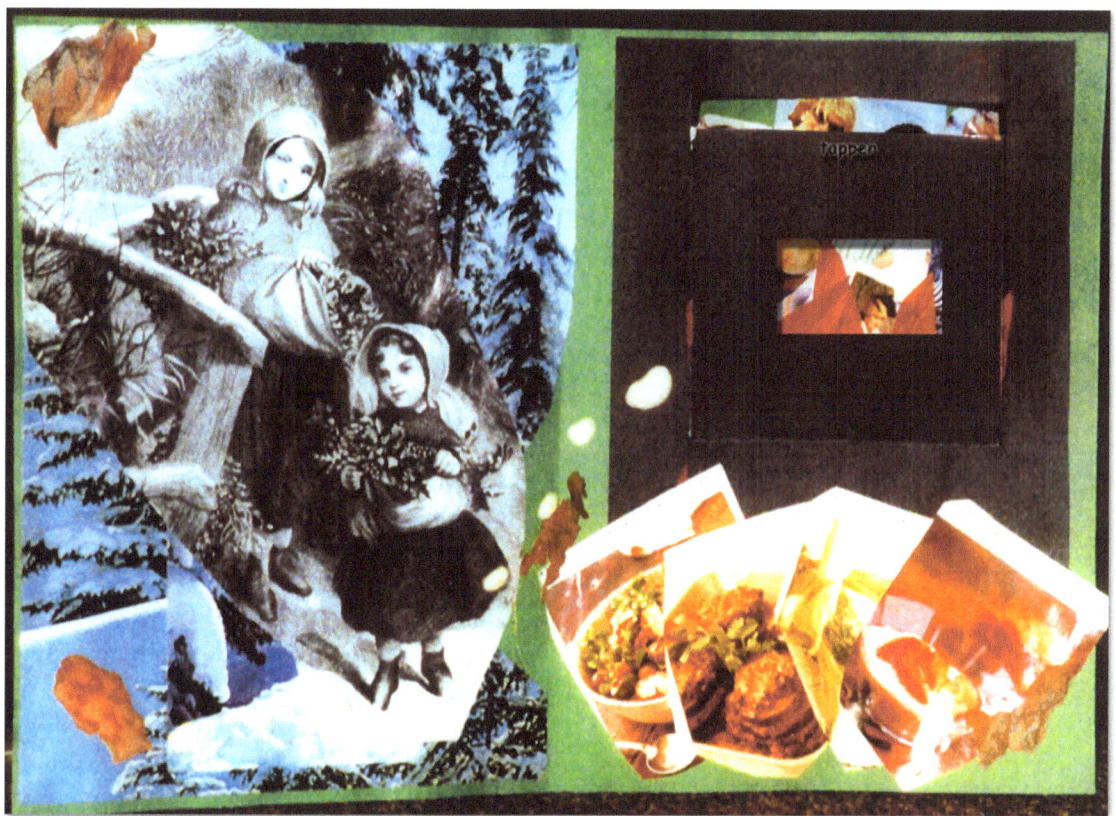

Part 2: Martha Lives! (shown here)

It was with great satisfaction that I cut the original composition apart and arranged the elements. Now Martha, the witch, is roasting in the oven while the children are safely finding their way back home. But wait… fairy tales may have happy endings, but true life rarely does. The Innocents may be free of Martha's grasp but this does not mean that the world has been freed of her forever. Like the Phoenix rising from the ashes, Martha is resurrected to become the guru of home decorating and gardening. Martha lives! My exultation gave way to resignation. Here is real life, not the fairy tale.

Two Young Girls Speak With Marcia:

Marcia: *How did you manage to come into the clutches of that overbearing, witchy woman Martha and how did you manage to get away?*

The Girls: *We were walking in the woods collecting greens to decorate our home for the Christmas holiday when we met this woman who seemed very nice and concerned about what we would do with our greens. When we told her we were just going to place them on our fireplace mantle and window ledges she seemed shocked. She told us there were many more glorious and delightful creations that could be made with our little bundles. Would we like to see some of her samples and learn how to do it ourselves? And she also offered us some hot minted chocolate cocoa. It all seemed so grand. So we walked with her and 150 odd other people who had been stripping green boughs from the trees to her home which was much larger than any we'd known.*

Marcia: *And what happened next? Were you afraid?*

continued on page 56

The Girls: *Oh no, she was so kind and so pretty and happy. She warmed the cocoa and served it to us in beautiful antique cups.*

Younger Girl: *But the saucers didn't match!*

Older Girl: *You should never have said that to her. That made her a little angry with us. She told us that truly lovely pieces don't need to match. They just need to harmonize with one another in an artful arrangement. Remember, all the cups, saucers and plates were blue and white.*

Younger Girl: *But they didn't match!*

Marcia: *And after the cocoa what happened?*

The Girls: *She took us to her workroom. It was the largest place you've ever seen with all kinds of tools. She showed us Christmas wreaths that she had been making. We'd never seen anything like them. Why... the pine cones were gold, not brown, and the berries and nuts too ...all dipped in gold! How it glistened. But somehow it wasn't real. Our Momma and Poppa would not believe a wreath with gold on it.*

Marcia: *But didn't you want to make one also?*

The Girls: *She started to show us how. First we needed to bend our boughs just so and twist them with wire. That hurt our fingers! Then she gave us the gold dipped pinecones, nuts and berries and told us that we'd have to put them on with a glue gun. That's when we started to be frightened of her. She plugged this small gun into the wall and filled it with opaque sticks. It smelled funny and hot. We thought it could burn us and our clothes. While she was in a closet getting more decorations, we shut her in and locked the door. Then we picked up our own bundles and ran away from the house. It was light outside so we were able to find our way back home.*

Marcia: *Were you glad to get back?*

The Girls: *Oh, yes! And our fresh boughs smell heavenly on the mantle and window ledges.*

CHAPTER SEVEN

Inward Journey: A Guided Fantasy

Enriching Expressive Art Using Visualization

Creativity is the real magic of the universe, because we have the power to envision something in our head, in the darkness, pick up any tool that we want, and create that. That is magic. We are conjurers and we need to see ourselves in that light.

—Adriana Diaz,
Freeing the Creative Spirit

Fantasies And Visualizations

Guided fantasies are another way to connect with the deeper parts of yourself. When the mind is quiet and the body relaxed, intuitive clarity is more accessible. Think of guided visualization as a gift to yourself, a mini-vacation, and a chance to enter another reality for a brief period of time. It helps you to relax and focus on what is important to you right now. Get ready to access your imagination. Take some time before beginning the visualization to make a quiet space by using candles, soft music, or silence and any other relaxing surroundings that appeal to you.

The following imagery can be used any time of year, but is particularly powerful when used at the beginning of winter. Read this to yourself or ask someone to read it to you slowly and quietly while you close your eyes and allow images to appear in your mind's eye.

The Colors Of Winter And The Fires Within

Take a few moments to close your eyes and to notice your breathing without changing it in any way. Notice your in-breath and out-breath and how the air fills your body and is released. Notice the temperature of the air

as it passes in and out of your nostrils and how your lungs expand and contract. Become aware of the sounds in the room and put all of your attention on them. If you use 100 percent of your focusing energy you will hear things you never knew were present. Now put your attention on your body and adjust yourself so that all parts of you are comfortable. Let each out-breath be a reminder to relax.

Summer's gregariousness and autumn's abundance are out of season now. We have cycled into a season of winter.

Winter's adventure is perhaps the greatest of all.

Winter is the most private of times from which can come a deepening and rebirth of the self.

As in the natural world, winter offers an opportunity to stop, to die back. In fact, it is essential, if life is to continue.

This is a time to take stock and to give the seeds of the coming season a chance to ready themselves.

Imagine that it is evening and you are alone, walking on a path through a winter field.

Look at the scene around you. Notice the temperature of the air and how it feels on your skin. Be aware of the scent in the air and the detail of the drying wild flowers and grasses. Be aware of the colors of all that meets your eyes.

You are at the edge of a forest now and you can see a path before you. The sun is low on the horizon and casts long shadows of the trees. The path beckons you. You take one last look at the field and turn to walk into the woods.

The path winds its way deeper and deeper and you're aware that you've never been here before. With each step, the silence grows and the darkness settles. There is darkness all around now and only tiny pinpoints of light show through the trees in the night sky.

It is becoming colder and the ground is covered in a blanket of crisp snow. The sounds of your movement along the path seem noticeable and distinct. Though it is hard to see the path, it is there for you. You wind your way into the forest deeper than you have ever been before. There is no end in sight.

You enter a clearing which has some light coming into it. Look around, take stock of your surroundings and notice a small cottage. You realize suddenly and with no doubt at all that this is your place. You make your way to the door and when you turn the knob, you find the door unlocked and opening. Inside it is warm and inviting. Look around in the light thrown by the crackling fire. What do you see? Are there others present? Wander about so that the details of this space become familiar. Make yourself comfortable. Settle in. Spend some time relaxing in the warmth and settle in for the night. Safely private and undisturbed, you begin to find your connection with a deep wisdom inside of yourself.

What does that part let you know?

What questions do you need to have answered?

What information do you get about what is important in your life?

In which direction do you need to go?

Do you need to let go of something?

As time goes by, you find yourself becoming drowsy and dreamy, and the next thing you know you awaken from a peaceful sleep.

Slowly, you arise. As you look through a frosted window, you realize that it is daylight.

You prepare to leave your cottage.

Do that in your own way.

Take something, if you wish, to symbolize any new or remembered insights or wisdom.

Trace your way back through the forest.

How is the trip different in the daylight? What do you see?

As you emerge into the field, let yourself see the beauty of the winter landscape: the bare trees against the horizon; the sunlight and the shadow; the unbroken winter sky.

Let yourself wander through the field.

Take a picture of it with your eyes and carry it back with you as you return slowly to your present location.

You know that far from being barren, this is a season of depth which hides a promise that roots will grow stronger and that streams will flow swiftly and birds will sing once again.

Expressing Your Experience

After returning to your awareness of the room, look through your collage materials and see how you can express this experience. When you are done, give your collage a title and converse with the parts of it. (See Chapter 1: Getting To Know Your Collage; and Chapter 2: Conversing With Your Collage.)

If you imagine yourself bringing back a walking stick as Lisa did (see *The Dark Bundle*), find a stick that fits your image and decorate it with yarn, ribbons, beads, feathers, bells, etc.

"Creative work is not self-indulgent.
It is not pointless or trivial.
It is crucial to our own healing
and the healing of our planet."

—Jan Phillips,
God Is at Eye Level

A Deep And Unknown Forest

The Journey

T'was a cold winter's night as I journeyed inward through a deep and unknown forest. With nothing more than dim starlight shining through the tent of branches, I stumbled forward. The silence was broken by the squeak of dry snow at my step as I tried to keep to the path. Faith kept me moving onward. Finally I entered a clearing and saw a rustic cabin I took to be my own. I entered.

Arrival

I am immediately blanketed with warmth from the fireplace. As my eyes adjust to the dim, golden glow I see and feel the presence of all the people who have loved me, both living and not. I am so needing to be with them right now. I have found the place to mend my heart a little while. I let myself be held and cared for. I take it in. I take in more. And more, and more. I keep my heart open to the love. Tears stream down my face as I soften and melt.

—Gale, 60's

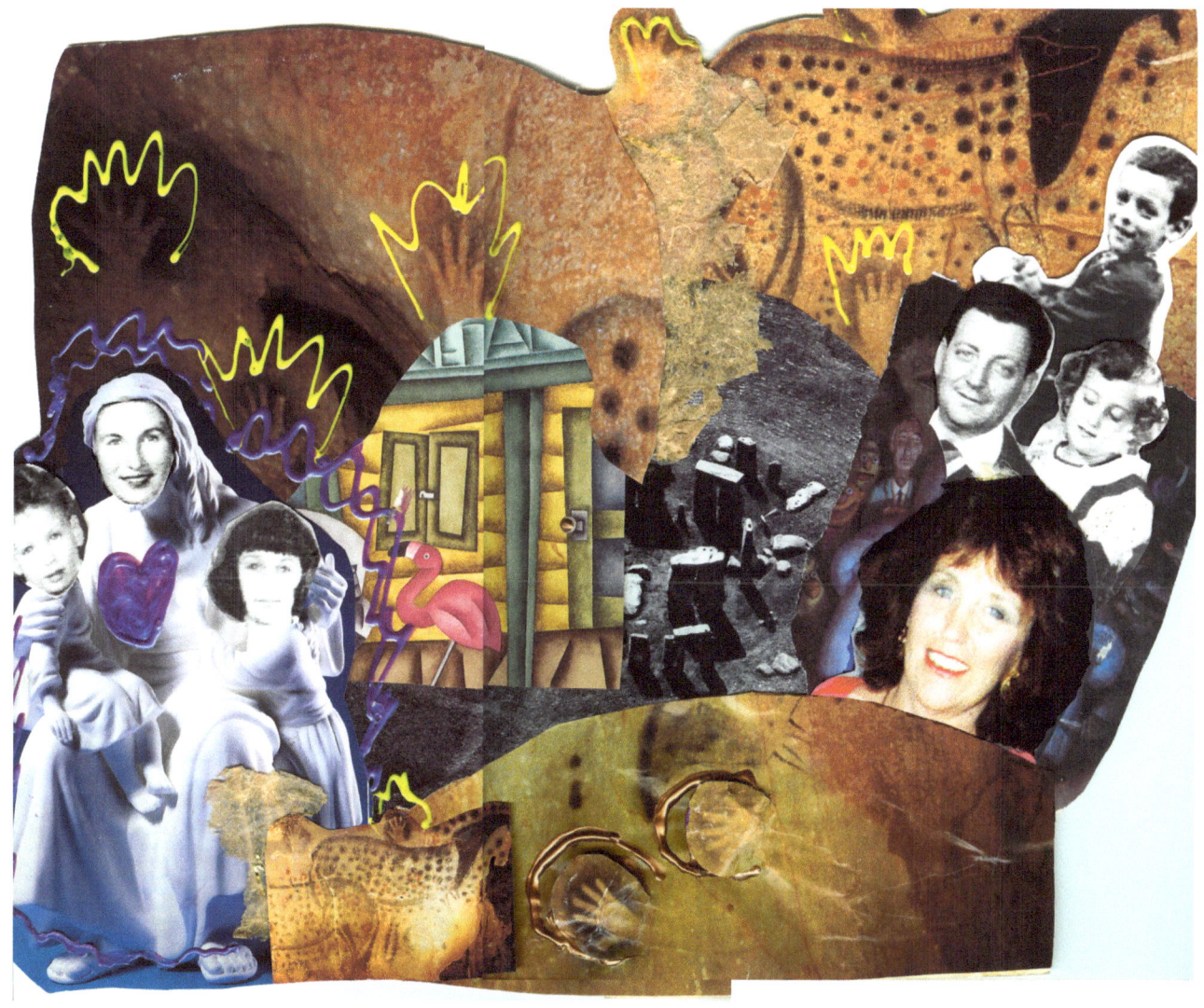

The Dark Bundle

It's a year later (since the collage was made) and I'm still on this Winter Journey. I put off writing about it, I think, because the journey doesn't end, doesn't even offer a resting point. It keeps going…forward…growing… Different stories roll in my path and blessings have grown and matured, fermented almost, into what will one day be sweet wine. Yet there is more I have wanted to hide in the dark bundle, too painful to realize their blessings.

My journey is to find those blessings, the stars shining in the darkness, and learn from each situation. My walking stick I took from my fantasy meditation. On it there is a shell near the bottom, reminding me to walk carefully and listen to the steps. It's also a reminder that I have strength. I have in myself a walking stick and the ability to find the blessings if I keep my eyes and ears open. I used the walking stick when I walked through the nest, all tangled and broken. The nest was my family, a confusing and tangled mess, ready to fall apart. As time would show me, the nest would fall apart and when it did, along with sadness and pain, I found blessings, unknown strengths inside of me. Looking back on the collage, I realize that it was a necessary part of my path, and I see glitter I had hidden in the nest has actually spread on the paper around it, as have the blessings in disguise in my life.

—Lisa, 20's

The Bundle

I thought I had been abandoned by goodness while I was inside the dark bundle, until I stepped back to see the blessings that grew out of darkness. The bundle represents a dark time in my life, one I wanted to leave behind forever, one I really couldn't bear to look back on. But it was still there no matter where I turned. I looked back finally, trying to destroy it, to tie it up and throw it away, and I saw gold. I saw beauty peeking out of the darkness. I saw beautiful things in myself that came from darkness. As time passed, I could look back and now I see the bundle as a gift. With my walking stick in my hand and my senses heightened from each dark tangle I've come through, I choose to be aware of each blessing that rolls, walks or drops like a bomb onto my path.

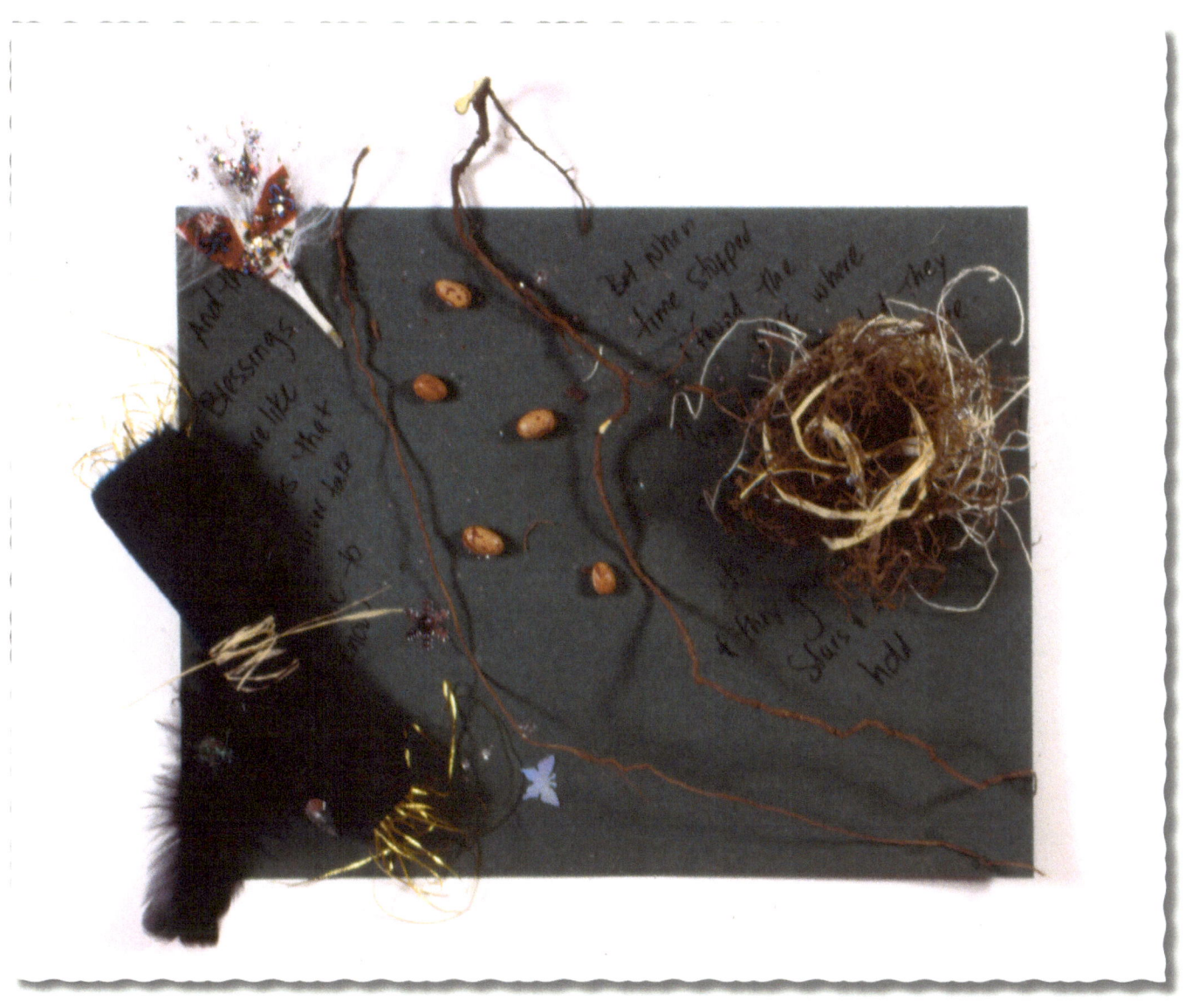

Words On The Collage:

The blessings were like poets that we never find time to know
But when time stopped, I found the place where lonely poets go
And they said, "Here have some coffee, it's straight, black and very old,"
And they gave me sticks and rocks and stars and all that I could hold.

—Dar Williams

Winter Art Show

Cabin:

Come to me. I await you. I offer respite and renewal; contemplation of what is most important. You must muster courage to get to me, must have faith that I will be here when you are afraid. Let go and come to me. I offer care of your heart and more.

Winter sun, Winter moon: (see below)

I am a light in the darkness and/or the grayness. Let me remind you of the beauty and stillness that is winter. Be outside to see me. Watch me through the trees as you walk through the woods. Remember how well you take pictures with your mind. Walk outside, take pictures.

Face Behind The Sun/Moon: (see opposite page)

I am tears and fears and preoccupation with worries. I keep you from being in the moment. I am often behind the scene, nagging, flinging out catastrophic thoughts. Don't ignore me, reassure me. Take me to the cabin. Do not allow me to run your show.

Face Dripping:

Today I am so fitting. Your home is leaking water and it is covering me, freezing me. This may go on for weeks, months, years. A grind of things to do to keep water/illness at bay. Sometimes you contemplate giving up. Your faith in the cabin wavers. Keep up with the work that needs to be done. Accept the labor of it. Do not dread it.

Ribbon:

I am your connection to breast cancer. Your mother, your sister, perhaps you some day, all the other women, the family members who have lost so much. All the fear, dread, pain. I am with you and this is good. Connections. Know also that you are supported by a very large and caring community.

—Susan, 60's

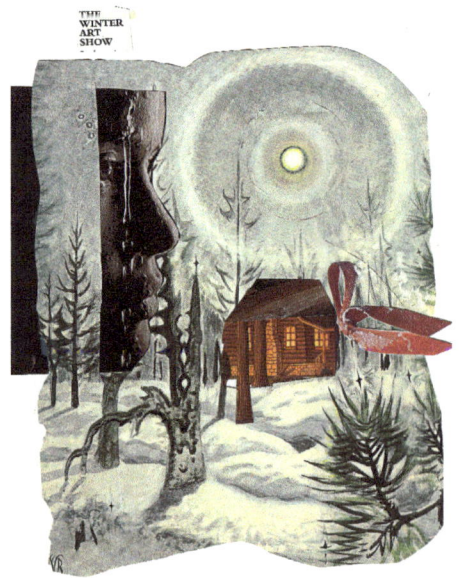

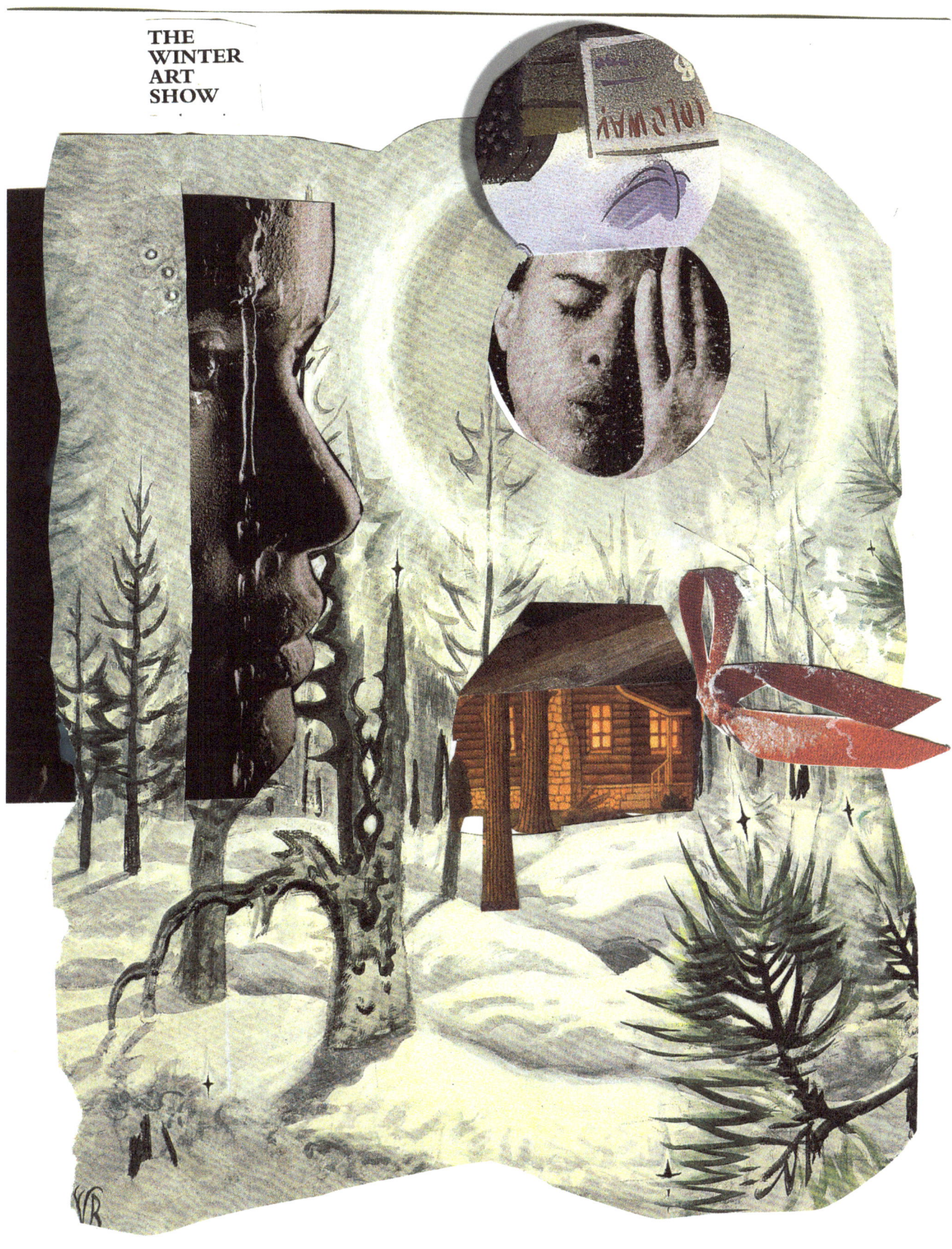

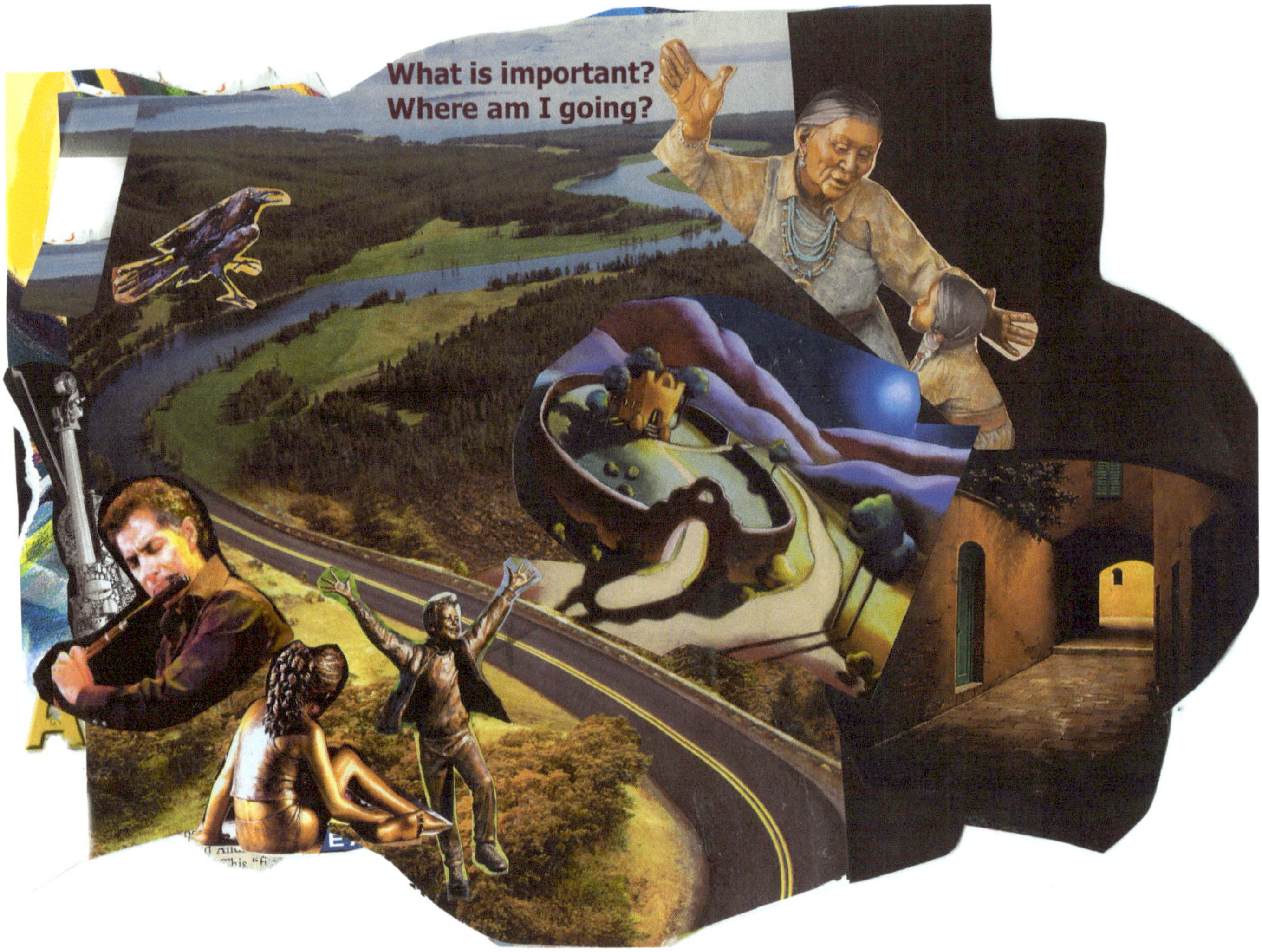

Even if you live to be 100, it's really a very short time.

So why not spend it undergoing this process of evolution,
of opening your mind and heart, connecting with your true nature
—rather than getting better and better at fixing, grasping, freezing, closing down?

—Pema Chodron

Butterfly At Daybreak

CHAPTER EIGHT

Sculptural Collage: Expanding Into New Frontiers

Expressing Your Emotions And The Meaning of an Experience Using Symbols And Three Dimensions

Imagination is more important than knowledge.

—*Albert Einstein*

Three-Dimensional Forms

Sculptural pieces refer to those expressive works done in three dimensions. Adding a third dimension can increase the depth of your expression or add an element of surprise or humor. In collage sculpture or construction, nothing is off limits. Sculptures can fit into the palm of your hand or be larger than you.

This chapter includes some collages crafted from very unique materials. The results are highly original and striking. Renee transformed a zip-lock bag and styrofoam balls into a uterus symbolizing her future. Gale used rusted junk and rotting wood from the grounds of an old farm and created an image of a passionate, aging woman, her breast an old faucet. These art pieces were not planned ahead of time. They emerged from a quiet moment of reflection. Both women set out only to find a way to express important personal information. We encourage you not to think ahead to a finished product but to stay with your feelings of the moment and move to the next step as your emotions move you.

Creating Your Sculpture

To begin, state a current feeling or concern or refer back to Chapter 2 to choose a topic for your exploration. Be spontaneous. Try unfamiliar materials. Once you have some ideas of what feelings or questions, thoughts or beliefs you want to express, search around your home or outdoors to find items that attract your attention. Then assemble your objects into a three-dimensional sculpture.

When you are finished, converse with your sculpture. (Refer to Chapter 2. You can also review the instructions in Chapter 1 for other ideas for getting to know and conversing with your sculpture.)

Dreams pass into the reality of action.
From the action stems the dream again;
and this interdependence produces
the highest form of living.

—*Anais Nin*

I Ain't Dead Yet

To face my aging process and accompanying fears of eventual decline I gave myself the assignment of making a piece of art from "found" objects I thought ugly. It was wrenching to select rusted tin cans and wire mesh, dead flowers and torn asphalt as I wandered around the farm. I was fully aware of my strong aversion to selecting such unattractive garbage.

My next step was to put these things together into a form/structure and I felt I had to decide whether I could justify beautifying it with paint and decorations. Yes, I thought, in life one can do that. Therein lies creativity. I selected stones to paint for mouth and eyes and decided that eyes in this body did not want to be able to see. I threw them out. I laughed out loud at what had miraculously become my breast: an old faucet (see below), rusted and no longer working which I covered with a rusty metal cap. As I worked and glued and painted and arranged I began to feel love for all these parts and the sculpture that had become me.

—Gale, 50's

Sculpture Speaks To Gale:

Hey, don't be ashamed of me. I love who I am. I'm proud of this breast, no longer operational. Once the giver of sustenance, what a proud reminder this breast of mine. Look at my beautiful dress; hand painted with care, not another one like it ever. How perfectly my head sits here crumbling in the face, still present and patched and delicate. Don't give up on me, don't grieve for me, God damn it. I ain't dead yet!

Gale Speaks To Sculpture:

No, you are not dead. Forgive me. I want to embrace your spirit and spunk and your originality. I want to remember to love your arrogance and self-appreciation. Thank you.

Later I grieved sorely for my missing eyes. How important my eyes are and how quickly and thoughtlessly I had tossed them away. How often do I neglect to use my eyes to make connections and to see beauty? I searched the area but could not find them.

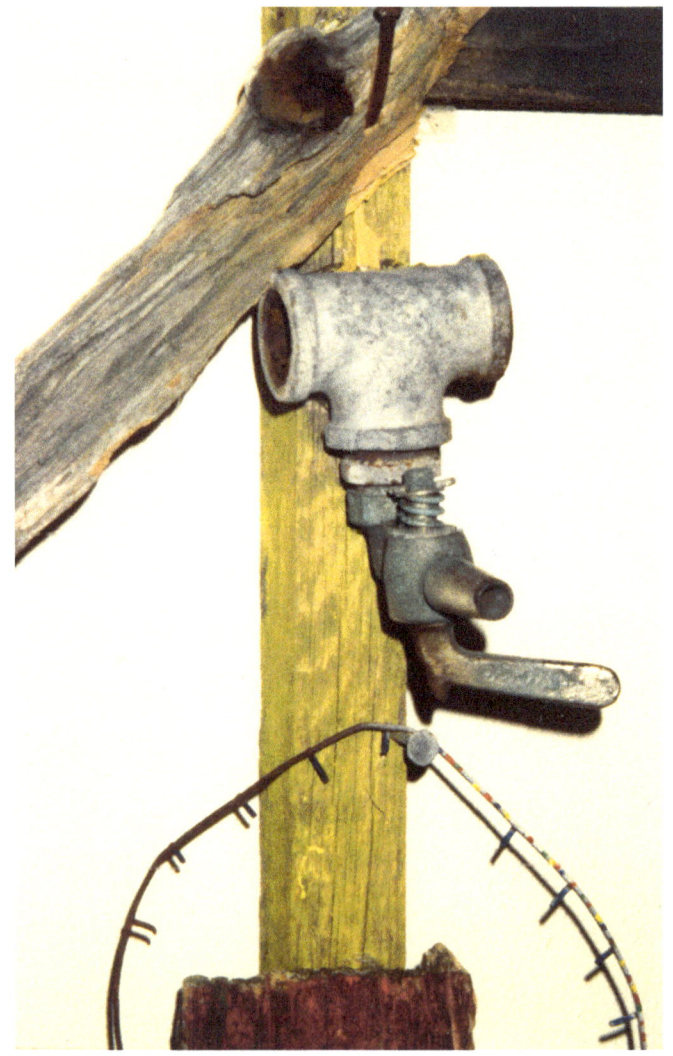

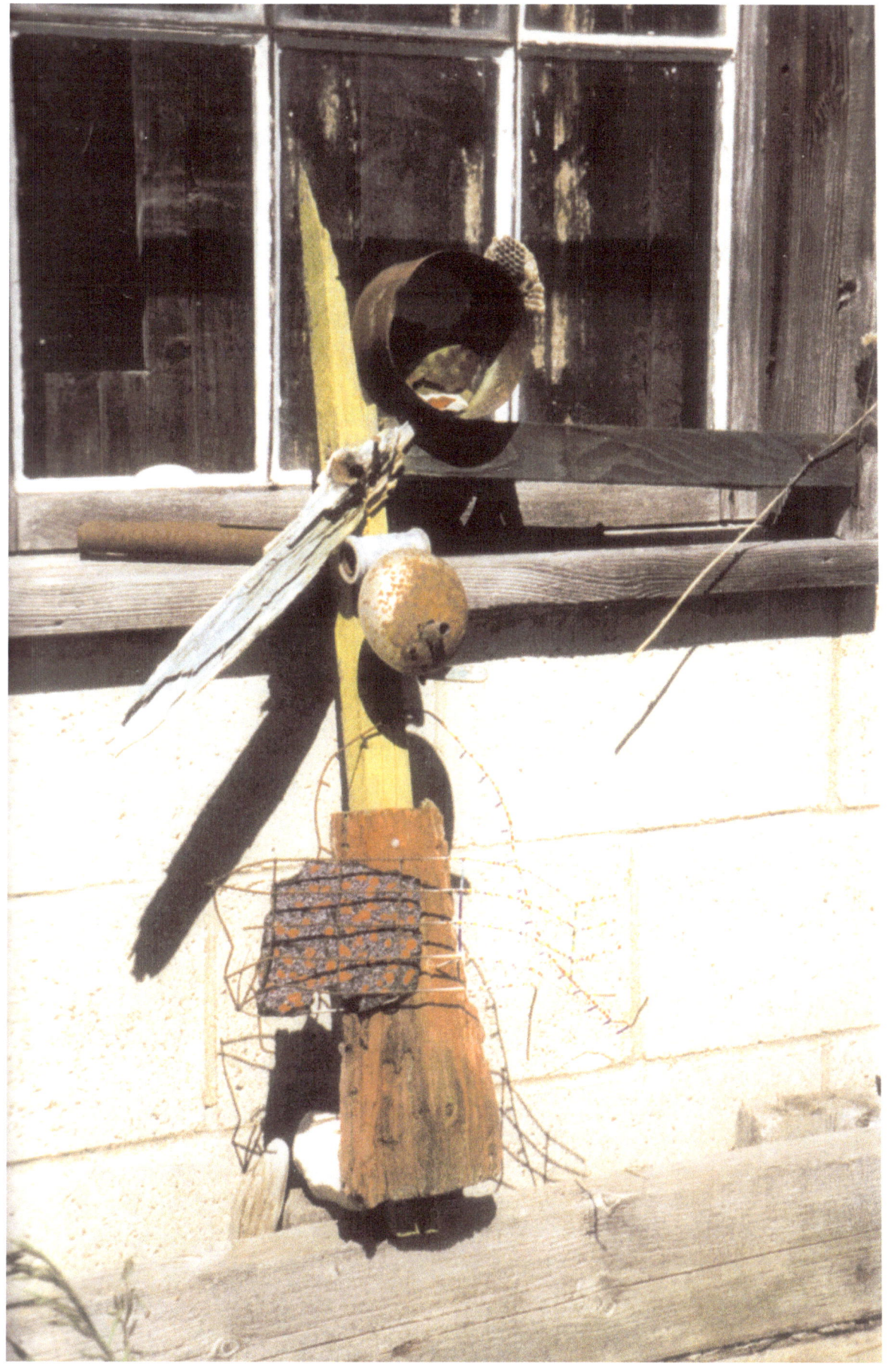

Celebrating The Womb Of Creativity

I had been monitoring fibroid tumors in my uterus for a number of years and was concerned about possible surgery to remove them if menopause did not occur in time to shrink them. Being in my late forties, menopause with its accompanying body changes and aging were also on my mind. The uterus is frequently seen as the center of creativity and my creativity was a quality that was extremely important to me and one I wanted to nurture. I decided to do something to celebrate my uterus as a way of expressing myself in this project.

First I needed to find something that would serve as a container into which I could put things. Looking through the materials available, a big freezer bag seemed ideal. (see p. 69) I began by decorating the outside. Since this was to be a celebration, I wanted it to be bright, shiny, colorful and happy. I also wanted to attach objects that would represent who I was. The brightly colored tissue paper, feathers and flowers served this function. The small sequin-like numbers and animals and plants represented my concern and interest in animal welfare, the environment and aging.

Inside the uterus (see p. 70) went my fears, hidden from view but still a powerful influence in my life. The fibroids were represented by small styrofoam balls and Spanish moss. Money worries, loneliness, where to live, growing old were other concerns that found their way into my uterus.

Suspended from the shiny garlands (this page) were my hopes and dreams for the future and they could be added to as time went by and as my needs changed. Right now I want to grow old unconventionally; no polyester or blue helmet hair for me. I found a picture of an older woman that represented the look I wanted. My desire for land with water on it was symbolized by a sea shell. A prayer for animals talked about my dream of having enough land for refuge for wildlife and a shelter for stray and abused cats and dogs. A cutout of a girl on a flying bird is attached so that I'll always have the freedom to be who I want to be.

—Renee, 40's

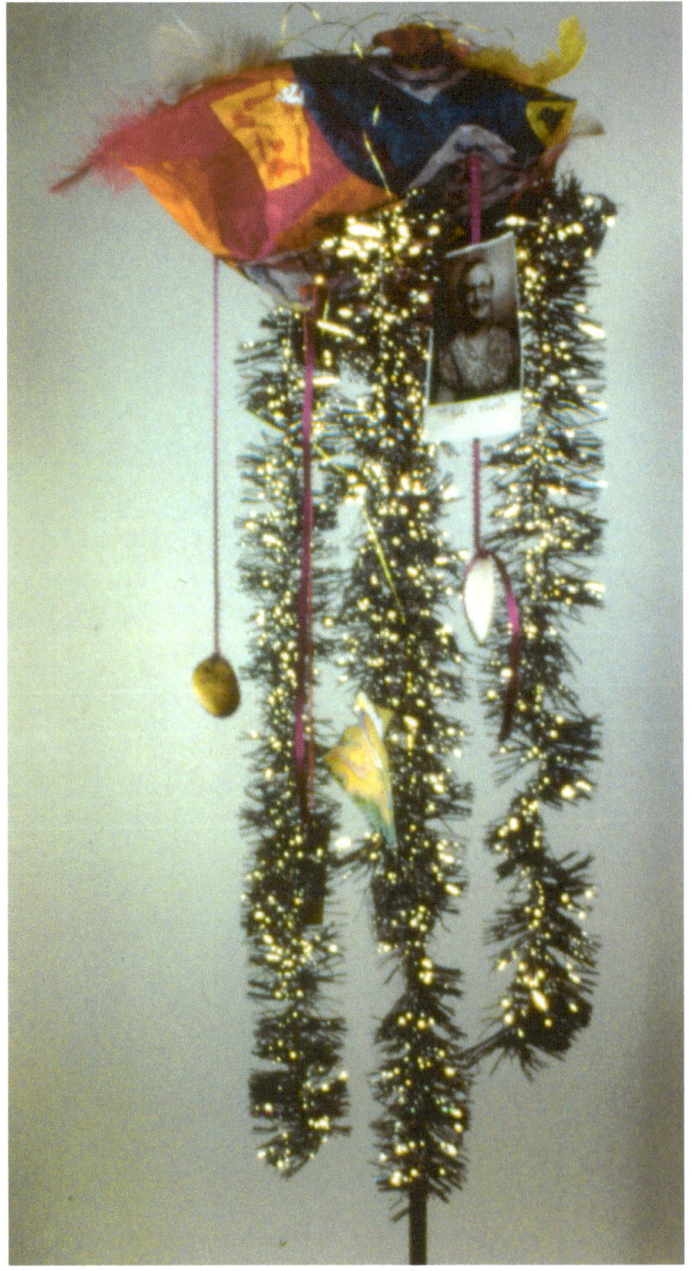

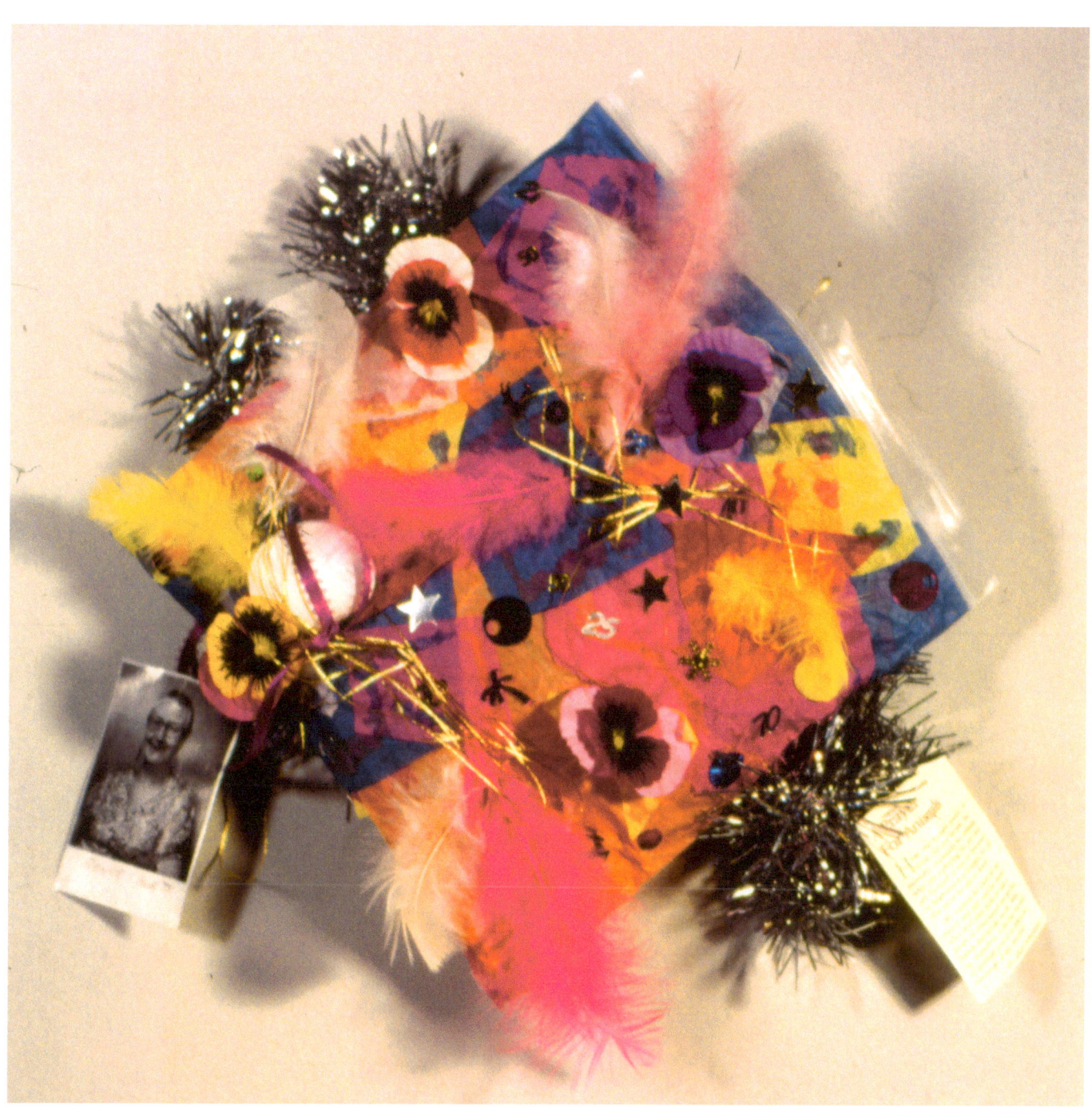

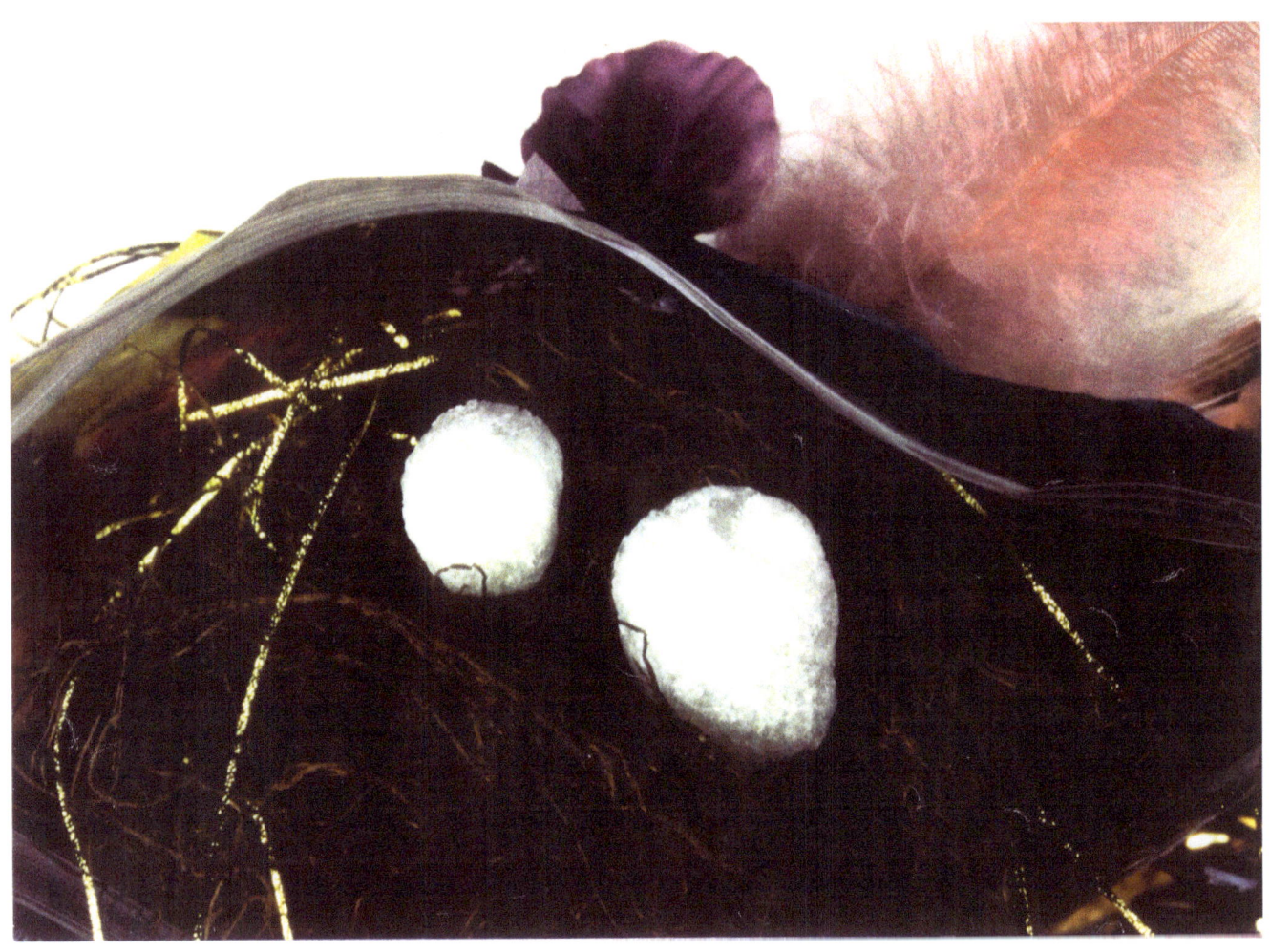

Postscript:

Four years after making this collage, I have purchased a home and barn on a large plot of forested land with a pond on it. More than a dozen stray and abandoned cats share the property with me.

Butterfly At Daybreak

CHAPTER NINE

Containers: Guarded Secrets And Surprises

Exploring What We Hide And What We Show To Others

All you need is deep within you waiting to unfold and reveal itself.
All you have to do is be still and take time to seek for what is within, and you will surely find it.

—Eileen Caddy, Co-founder of Findhorn Community, Scotland

Decorating Your Container

Containers of all sorts are useful in constructing collages. Boxes and bags of all sizes and shapes can be decorated inside and out, and objects placed inside can represent aspects of yourself.

A container can be decorated or collaged on the outside to represent your "public self"—those parts of you which are noticed or which you choose to show to those around you. The inside can be decorated or collaged to represent your "private self"—those parts of you unseen by others or seen only by those you trust and allow into your private life. You can be selective as to who may view this inner box or bag and under what circumstances. The container thus serves as a protective covering for the more vulnerable aspects of yourself.

Another option is to decorate the inside of a container to represent the total you or your total personality. These boxes are often referred to as "self-portrait" boxes. The outside surface can be decorated in any style you wish. Once again, you can be selective as to which audience is allowed entry into this secluded and protected space.

Containers can also contain images and craft materials which can represent your feelings or personal history such as memories.

Another option is to decorate the outside of the box only, each side representing a particular part of a theme. For example, each side might represent one of the four seasons, or one of the Native American "Six Directions."

"Me" Boxes

We have used "Me" boxes with children as young as eight years old. Kids are generally delighted to have this protected space to harbor special items, which represent them and speak to their current interests. Some children are better than others at using collage images to decorate the inside of their containers, but all have enjoyed discovering various ways to use colored tissue paper and liquid starch to decorate the outer surface. One very shy eight-year-old girl, a member of a domestic violence treatment group, was able to speak freely in an animated manner for the first time after many weeks of meetings, while showing her "Me" box to other members of her group. **We frequently notice how expressive art pieces can provide something to focus on and talk about for those who ordinarily feel too shy to speak in a group.**

We are intrigued by the element of surprise when a nondescript box opens to show great depth and beauty. The boxes explore the notion that one cannot too easily be judged by what shows on the outside.

After you have decorated your container, enjoy it. You can converse with each image or item you've selected to put into your container. You can also converse with the container as a whole.

We have to realize that a creative being lives within
ourselves whether we like it or not,
and we must get out of its way for it will give us
no peace until we do.

—*M.C. Richards*

In the greatest confusion there is still an open channel to the soul.
It may be difficult to find because by mid-life it is overgrown…
But the channel is always there, and it is our business to keep it open,
to have access to the deepest part of ourselves.

—*Saul Bellow*

Happiness Box

My "Happiness Box" is a statement of my coming into maturity, both the blooming of my femininity (the pink colors) and in my reconnection to God and Christ and to my true self. I've always collected angels, but now I realize they are just messengers and that I can go straight to the Source for true knowledge. Pictures on the outside tell my family history back to a great-grandmother who was part Blackfoot Indian. My granddaughter and I made the feathery pens. The contents of the box each have a story to tell of learning, healing, family and blessings.

—Sharon, 50's

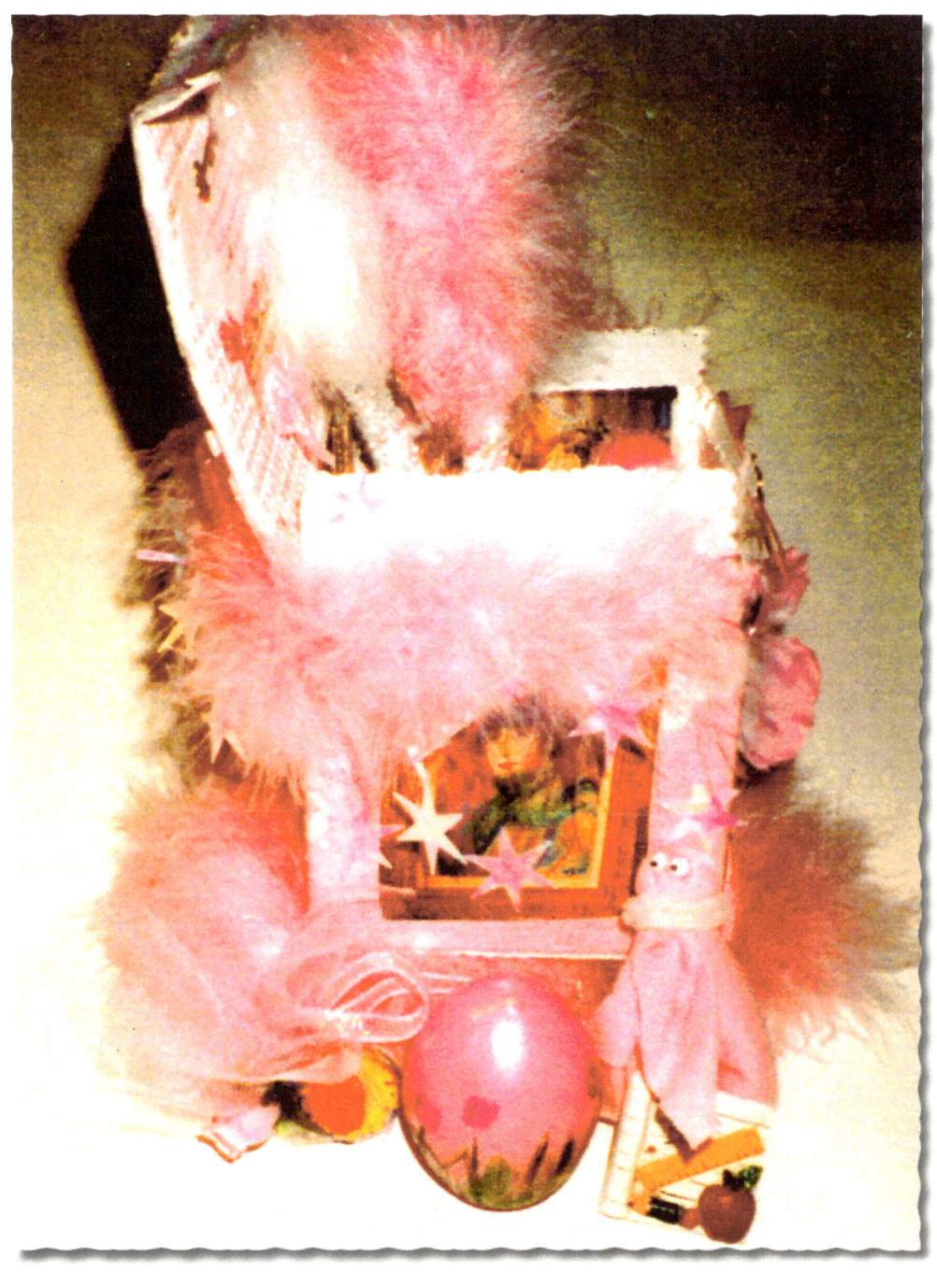

In The Bag

It was fun to paste pictures of things that I love on the outside of the bag (the outer or public me). I loved coloring the bag with brightly colored oil pastels. The inside wasn't difficult as I feel I'm quite aware of my internal being (the inner or private me).

The seascape side of my bag is my experience with snorkeling in the Bahamas, and most recently in Hawaii. When I'm in the ocean, I feel at peace with myself. The colors and shapes that I see are so varied as well as beautiful.

—JoAnne, 40's

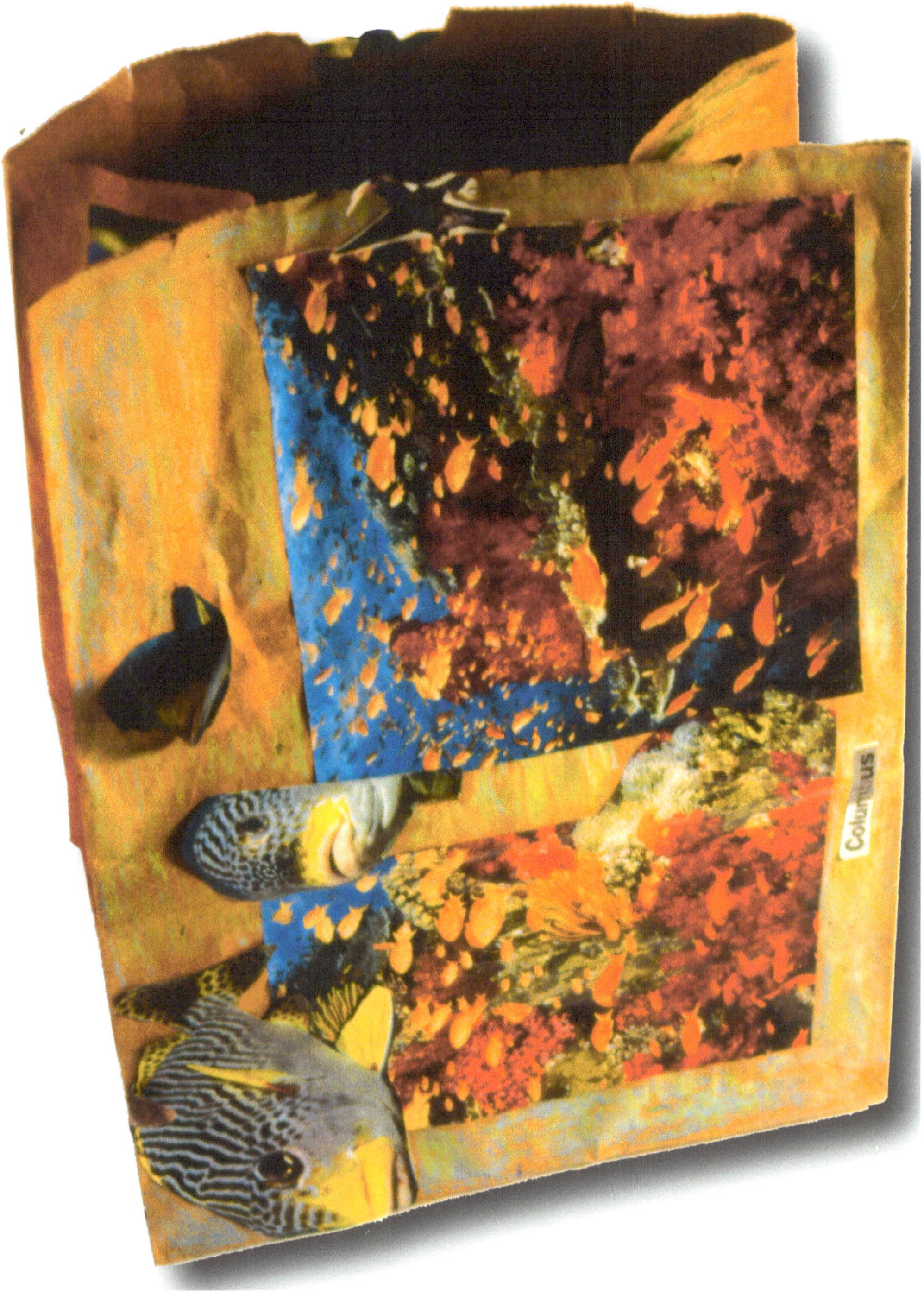

Out Of The Box

Out of the Box developed from my frustration of feeling too contained by this small box. I ripped it open, refusing to stay within its original boundaries. The door speaks to a phase of new "openings" in my life as well as my activities at Wellness House, providing supportive services to people with cancer. The birch bark represents my childhood growing up in Sweden. The finished box exhibits a lot more "wildness" than I had anticipated. I constructed this at a workshop integrating spirituality and expressive arts, and its open shape represents a cross.

—Eva, 50's

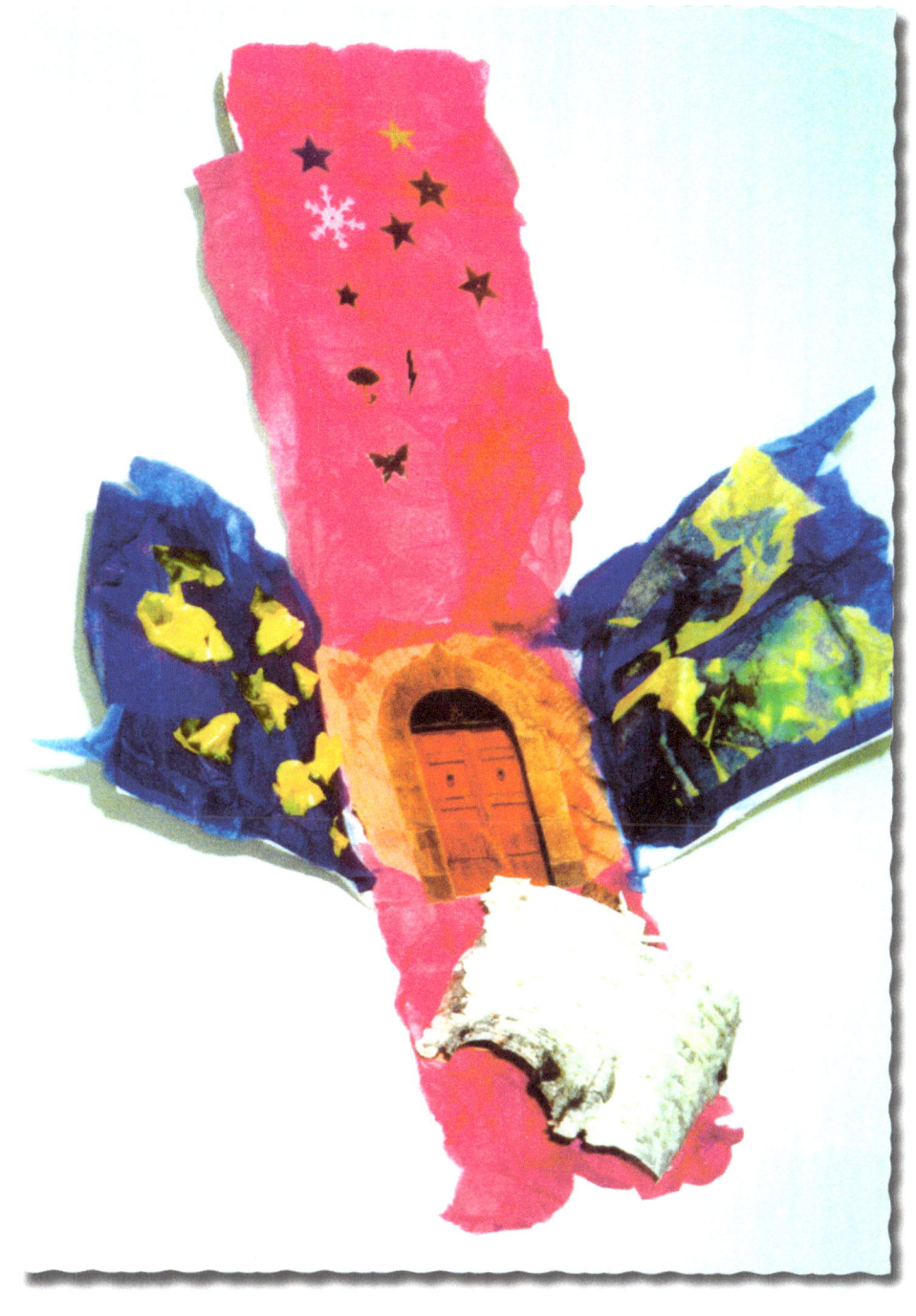

A Wrinkle In Time

I enjoyed covering my box with colored tissue paper which wrinkled like the wrinkles I'm accumulating. I'm not yet at peace with them. The feather and heart on the top of the box remind me to live with my heart in the lead and to allow myself to be guided by Spirit. Images on the inside of the box speak to the wisdom I've gained with and from my partner of 30 years, my quest for knowledge, my search for a "path with heart" and my process of good self-care.

The items inside my box, sitting in a nest of green grass, include a turtle (my reminder to move slowly), an egg (a symbol of new possibilities), and a strip of correction tape from my typewriter which reminds me that I'm okay even when I make mistakes.

—Ginny, 50's

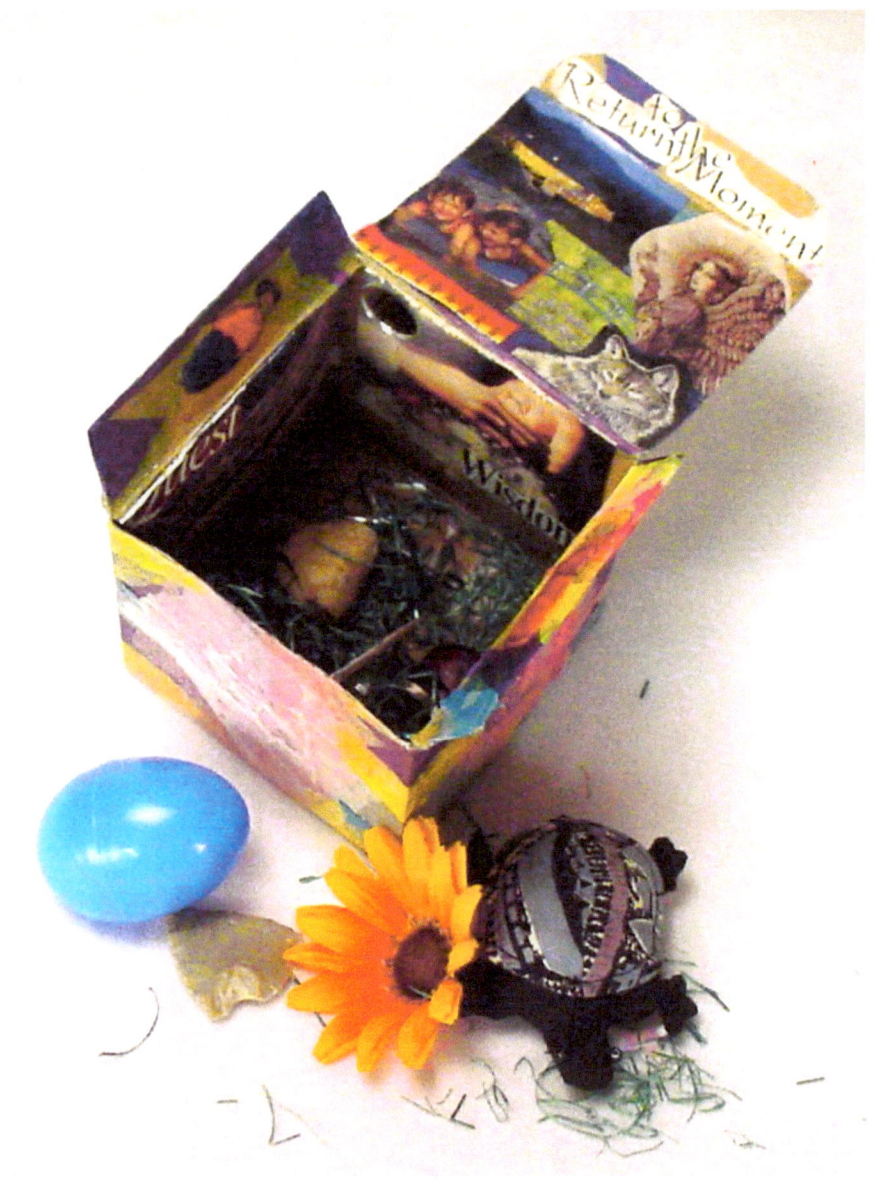

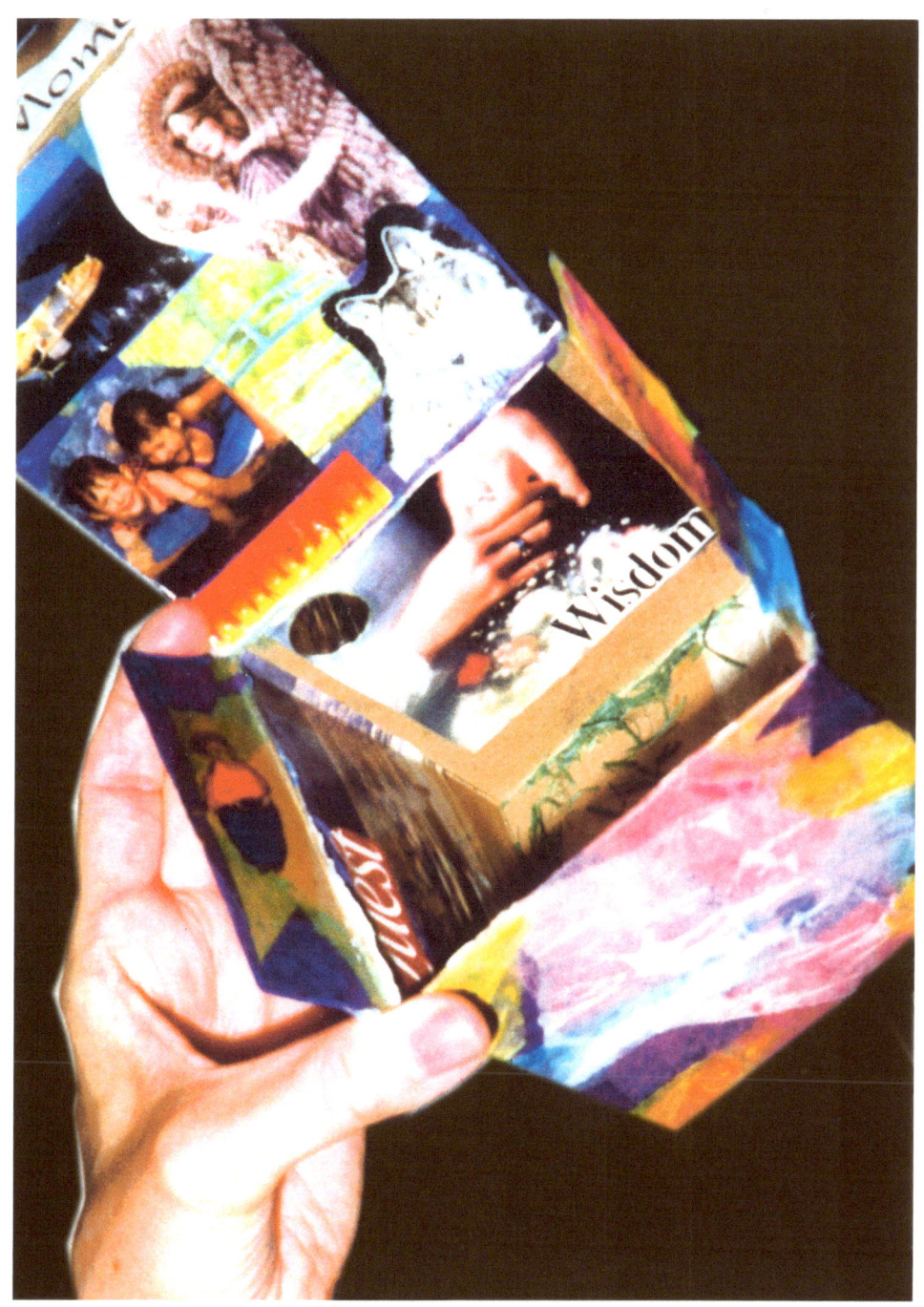

Celebrate Freedom

Celebrate Freedom is a tribute to South Africa where I grew up and the images speak to my newfound freedom in the enjoyment of expressive arts, especially collage journaling and photography. The orange lump on the side of the box represents the bumps I've encountered on my life path.

Now several months later, an image placed inside of my box of a framed picture decorated with crosses, big and small, has taken on a new meaning.

When originally placed in the box, it represented my strong faith. Looking at it a few weeks ago, I was struck by the creativity of the images, and I decided to collect crosses. Today, I am reflecting on the meaning and symbolism of "crosses" in my life, thinking about crossroads I've encountered, and crossings I've made and my current process of cross-examining my life.

—M., 40's

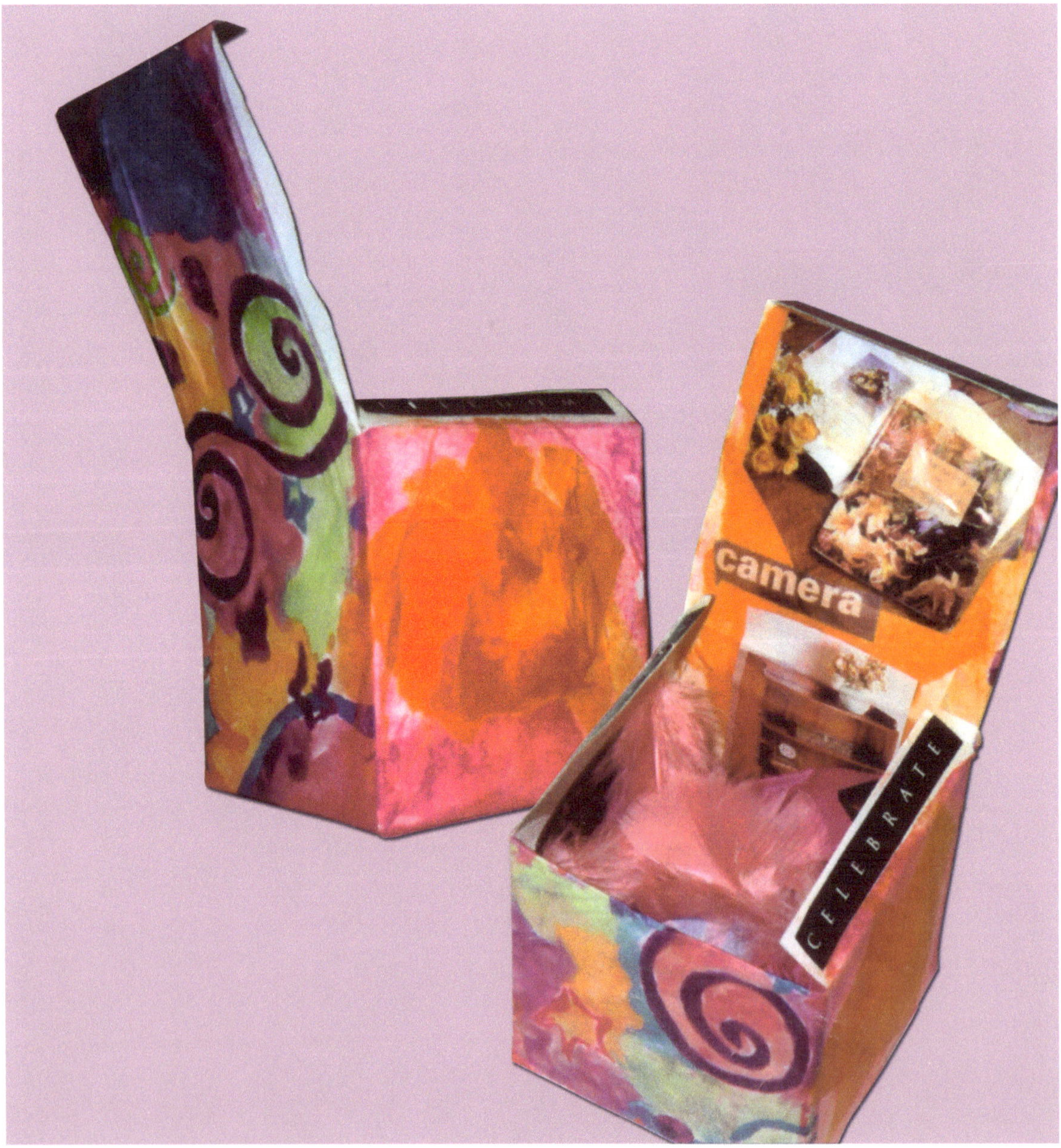

CHAPTER TEN

Making Peace With Our Bodies

Body Tracings And Masks

The body is a sacred garment. It's your first and last garment; it is what you enter life with and what you depart from life with, and it should be treated with great honor.

—Martha Graham, Dancer and Choreographer

Tracing Your Body

Using a tracing of your body as a canvas for your collage making can help you reconnect with and care for your body. Sometimes you may need to literally step back from your body in this way to see it more clearly. Making and decorating a body tracing is a unique way of looking at who you are and what you need.

Have someone who feels safe trace you with crayons or magic markers. Any type of paper can be used for your body tracing. Several sheets of white flipchart paper can be taped together to provide a surface of sufficient length and width. The tracing can be done with the paper on the floor or table or taped to a wall. A person can lie flat or on her side, with arms at the side, overhead, behind, or crossed in front. The legs can be arranged in any fashion. (Some of the children we've worked with have envisioned themselves as ice skaters, or basketball players shooting a basket.) The process of arranging and tracing your body can stir up many thoughts and feelings. It is important to pause after tracing your body to talk or think about how this activity felt for you and to talk about feelings which may arise.

How did it feel to have your body traced?

As you look at your tracing, what are your first impressions?

Is this larger or taller than you see yourself?

Smaller or shorter?

Hang it on the wall if you like and see how it looks to you. Look at it up close and then stand back and look at it. Do you look more or less powerful than you thought you looked?

From here you can choose one of several directions. Pick one that feels comfortable or one that draws your interest and would lead you to information you want to know.

A Body Self-Portrait

How could you embellish your tracing so that it would tell a viewer who you are and who lives in your body? Find ways to express your likes, dislikes, things you do, your values and any other part of you that you want to include. When you are done, take some time to have your tracing introduce itself to you. You can sit it on a chair and seat yourself across from it to carry on a conversation. Perhaps it has wisdom to share or feelings of anger, sadness, fear, or joy to express.

A Vision Of Wellness Portrait

After tracing your body, take time to scan your body and to notice which parts need special tending. Find images that offer healing to those places. Different parts may call out for different images.

Ginny filled her tracing with the most beautiful and soothing images from nature that she could find. Her body tracing reminds her that spending time outdoors is essential for her physical and emotional well-being.

Gale used magic markers to draw her body. On the front side she colored the parts that were uncomfortable or needing attention. Then she turned the drawing over and transformed it into a healthier, vibrant image. Have your tracing speak back to you as though it was already transformed. For example, "I have legs that are made of giant redwood trees. I can carry great weight with little effort." Continue on this way until all parts have had their say.

Body Image And Awareness

After tracing your body, **take time to scan your body, noting areas you criticize and noting which parts of your body you celebrate freely.** Highlight these areas of your body in various ways using craft materials, pictures, photographs, images or markers. Prepare for some discomfort. Pay attention to what you feel.

Ask the parts of your body (especially the parts toward which you may feel negativity) what they bring into your life that is worthwhile. For example: one woman used a board across the chest area of her body tracing to represent always feeling as "flat as a board." Her dialogue led her into more tolerance for her small breast size and appreciation for the way they had provided for her children and given pleasure to her spouse. One woman highlighted with collage, drawings and words all of the areas of her body that she judged to be imperfect based on what women are being told by the advertising media. She hardly had room to fit in all the negative messages: imperfectly colored nipples, no half moons on her fingernails, eyebrow hairs out of line, creases on her knees, an "outy" bellybutton, larger tops to her thighs, and the list went on and on. She began to think about what her body wanted and not about what advertisers wanted. She came to accept and appreciate her body as it is.

Dealing With Health Challenges

If you have an injury, pain, or other physical challenge, find a way to express that on your tracing. Then choose images that would feel healing to the parts of your body that need it. For example, a sprained ankle may need a soak in a luxurious Jacuzzi. Relief from aches and pains all over may conjure up images of floating in warm water with gentle ripples and currents. What can your pain tell you about how to reduce it or make peace with it or focus away from it? For example, if your knee has been aching, ask your knee to really honestly speak, even cry, about the pain. Ask it what would help. Ask it what it needs.

If you are dealing with a disease or infection, imagine how the infection operates in your body. Describe that in words or drawings or images on your tracing. Then find images that would facilitate the healing process.

When you talk to you body's parts they often will give you very clear, strong messages about what they need from you.

Start the conversation and let those parts talk about themselves and what it is like to be in your body.

Then ask this body part what it contributes or would like to contribute to your welfare. Then ask it what it needs from you.

Masking And Unmasking Your True Self

Another way to explore your body is to **create a mold of your face to form a mask.** Mask making allows you an opportunity to explore the ways in which you present yourself to the public or sometimes hide yourself from public view. From early history to modern times, from culture to culture, masks have fascinated us. They have been used in theatre arts to represent human qualities such as joy, evil, lust and greed.

They have been created in the likeness of well-known religious or political figures and worn to represent them, sometimes in protest or disagreement. When the wearer is hidden, she or he could feel constrained and unnoticed or incredibly free and spontaneous without the bonds of conventional standards, roles and class. To the viewer, a mask worn by another can be intimidating or intriguing. Making a mask provides an excellent opportunity to explore themes of self in relation to others.

Directions For Mask Construction

We follow the directions on the package of a plaster gauze product called Rigid Wrap, which can be purchased at most craft and supply stores. We prefer to use **3 layers** of plaster gauze. We also prefer to place a small square of paper towel over the eyelid and eyebrow to prevent water and plaster from getting into the eyes while applying the plaster gauze strips. Be sure to follow the instructions about the application of Vaseline to the face and hairline.

We allow the person to sit for about 5 minutes after the third layer of gauze is applied before gently wiggling the face and slowly and gently removing the mask.

Some people are more comfortable leaving the eyes uncovered during the application of the gauze strips, with the option of covering over the eye holes after the mask is removed from the face. Some also prefer to leave the mouth uncovered, or even wide open for effect. Always leave the nostrils open.

People who have suffered sexual abuse or other trauma may prefer not to do this exercise, may prefer to do it in the presence of a therapist, or may choose to purchase a ready-made mask to decorate.

The mask can be removed at any point in the process of application should the person feel uncomfortable or anxious. (See also *Maskmaking* by Carole Sivin for illustrated instructions for making plaster gauze and many other types of masks.) **Do not discard the water in your sink or toilet as the plaster can harden and necessitate a visit from your plumber!**

After the molded masks are removed from participants' faces, we like to talk about the many feelings that are stirred up by the process of applying the plaster gauze. We often ask participants, "What was this experience like for you? What feelings and thoughts arose during the process? Were you able to communicate your needs to others while the plaster was on your face? What did you learn about yourself from this activity? How did you feel working with your partner(s)?"

You can dry your mask overnight before decorating or dry it quickly in a microwave oven (see package directions). Plaster gauze masks can be colored with many types of paint and with any decorations, which can be attached with glue or a glue gun. Some people also decorate the inside surface of their masks. The natural imperfection of the gauze surface celebrates the distinctiveness of your face.

After your mask is decorated, you can converse with your mask. Ask it to tell you about itself, and ask it to tell you what the colors and decorations represent. Ask yourself what feelings arose during the decorating process, what you learned about yourself from the process and which aspect of yourself the mask represents, if any.

Masks Can Represent Many Aspects Of Self:

- True self
- Angry self
- Playful self
- Hidden self
- Child self
- Fearful self

- Public self
- Wise woman
- Shaman, or healer self
- Goddess
- Sexy self
- The Mother

- Wild self
- The Rebel
- Male self
- The Inner Critic
- Female self

Place the mask over your face and note how you feel about that. Imagine wearing your mask in front of others and imagine how others might react to it. Whichever aspect of yourself you choose to explore, make friends with your mask. You can ask it how it contributes to your life and how it keeps you safe.

There is a connection between self-nurturing and self-respect.
　　　　—Julia Cameron, The Artist's Way

*How many times
in a life
do we shed
yet another
chrysalis?*

　　　　—Sharon Gilbert

A Clear New Day

To trace my body, I chose to take a different pose from the usual (arms flat at sides) and chose a protective pose, with my arms crossed over my chest and my legs crossed at the ankles. Looking at the completed image, I decided it looked like a mermaid, so I made it into one by drawing a mermaid tail. My hair flows out from my head in waves.

I think the eyes are the most important feature. We learn a lot by looking through our eyes. I chose eyes that looked worried, aged. They have been through a lot, in contrast to my own young eyes. The expression, "A Clear New Day" felt inspirational to me.

—Laura, teens

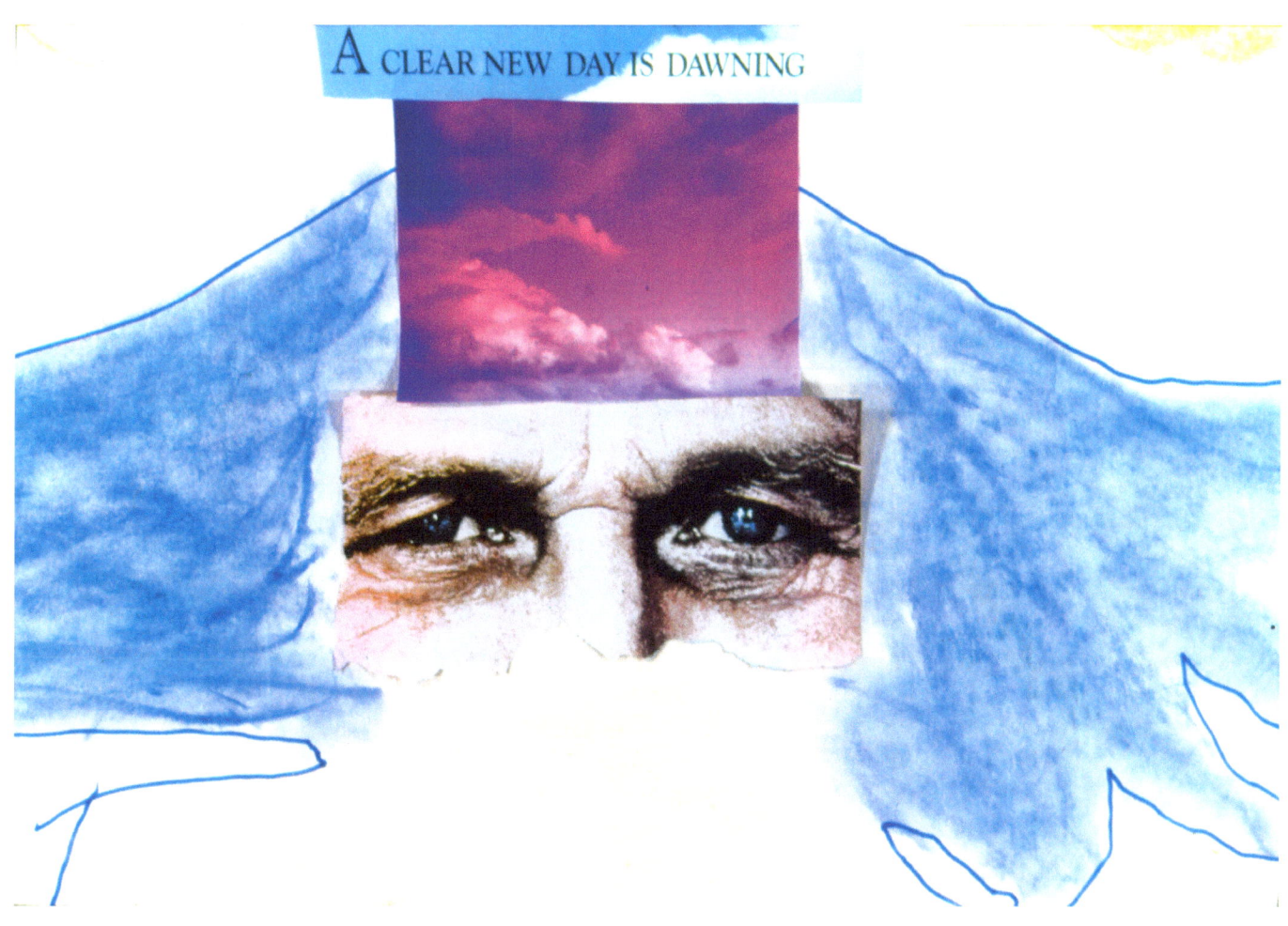

Body Beautiful

I'm a highly sensitive person, or HSP, according to author Elaine Aron, Ph.D. in her book, *The Highly Sensitive Person*. One of my favorite ways of unwinding and replenishing my energy is to spend time outdoors.

I decorated my body outline with images which I find soothing and restful and images of some animal friends. Butterfly represents transformation and is placed over my heart. The roses and yellow bird on my head represent the wonderful music and sweet scents I crave when out-of-doors. My only concession to winter is my belt, an image of gorgeous ice crystals. I reach out with my hands to the heavens in appreciation of this fragile endangered planet.

I hung this life-size poster on my bedroom door. When I turn on the fan it dances!

—Ginny, 50's

Body Speaks To Ginny:

I am your body. I may be sensitive, but I am not fragile! I came here with a job to do and I plan to stay here until I am finished. I respond well to loving treatment, and you and I need to maintain regular communication. I can tell you what you need to know. You need just ask. I am coming back into balance. All your hard work is beginning to pay off. We will feel better—for many years. We will experiment until we find the best way. We make a good team. Mind and body with spirit in the lead!

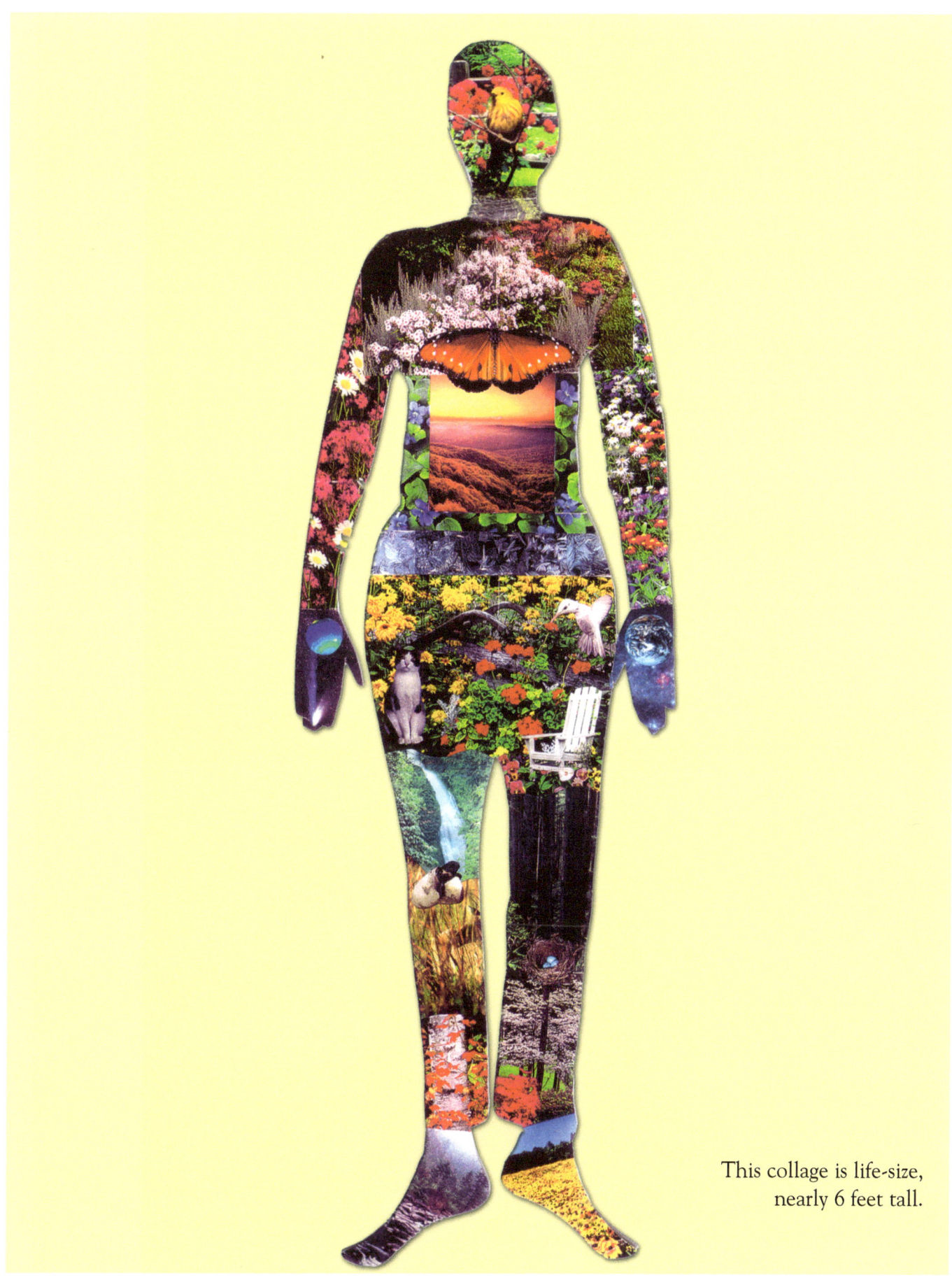

This collage is life-size,
nearly 6 feet tall.

Dragonfly Woman

When I was being treated for depression and was very despondent one of the therapists helped me to realize that the colors yellow and green were very healing for me. I used them on the mask on my forehead and eyes. Yellow represents the sun and its warm rays. Green is my favorite color. It's restful and peaceful.

The dragonfly on top of my crown represents my struggle to become a functioning, stronger woman.

Emerging from the top of my head, freeing itself from all the painful memories, it is flying for a new life. Now that it knows so much more, I have turned it around to fly back into my head to bring in new awareness and more strength to my wild woman and to help me develop a richer, more meaningful life.

—JoAnne, 40's

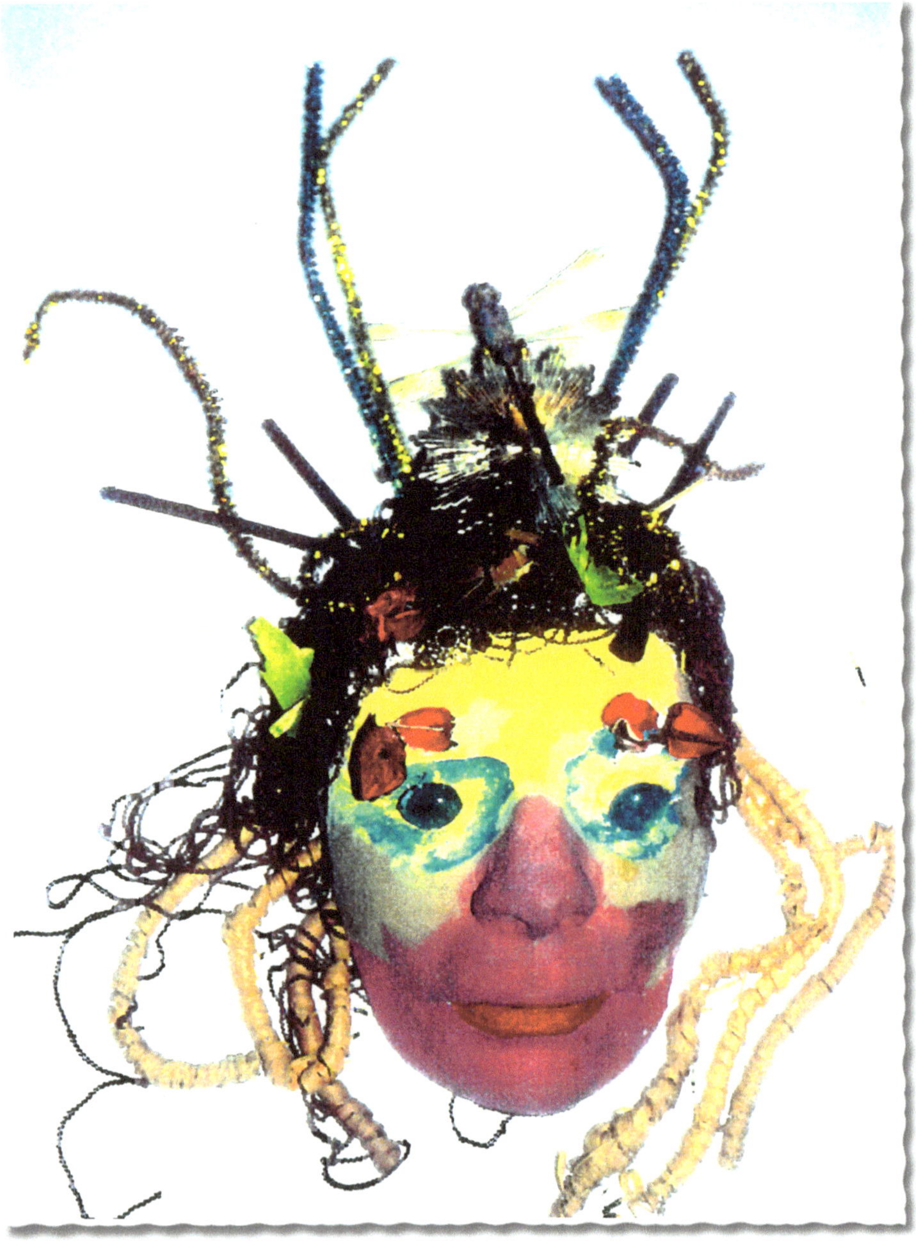

My Grandmother's Face

I felt safe with my friend Melissa applying my mask, talking to me gently as she touched my face. As she began to cover my face, however, I thought back to a traumatic, suffocating event, and I began to panic. I calmed myself by reminding myself to be in the present, and the whole experience turned out to be cathartic for me, letting go (with some tears) of the original trauma. When I got my first look at the mask, I didn't recognize myself! What I saw instead was my grandmother's face and we're not related biologically. I was frightened initially, looking at the "true self" that my mask represents, but I soon felt calm and serene and began to chuckle at the sight of my squished-up nose.

I chose the color pink for the feminine part of me which I had been unable to express in my profession of preventing theft in the marketplace. On the job, I had to be the "tough guy." I enjoyed pulling together the dramatic decorations. My eyes shine with jewels of wisdom. Making the mask produced a lot of peace for me and I'm still processing it.

—Sharon, 50's

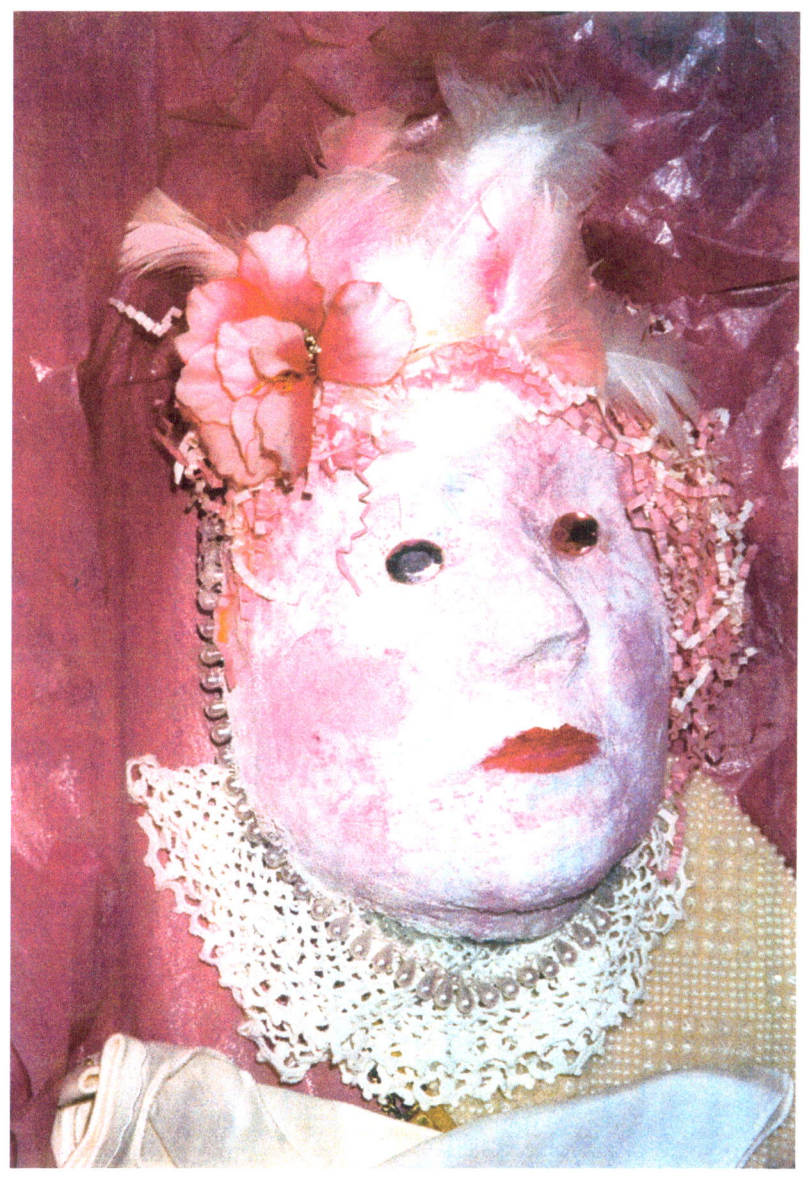

Making Peace With Our Bodies

Facing Myself

With some degree of surprise I faced my near likeness when I removed the plaster cast from the alginate mold. (See your dentist for further instructions. Gale had the bright idea to use the powder he had mixed up so often to make all those perfect but unwanted dental impressions.)

I wanted to decorate this cast but how would I limit my creative expression with so rich a lifetime and so many collage materials at hand?

I chose to divide the face into two parts: youth and aging.

Finished, finally I sat with my face and conversed with it.

—Gale, 50's

Age Speaks To Youth:

How lovely you are and how much fun you were to dress. Bright colors and shiny baubles, ribbons and gold. You are bouncy and buoyant and busy, flying free.

Youth Speaks To Age:

How beautiful you look to me. So much a part of the natural world. You have volume and substance and richness of color. Your textures keep my eyes engaged and invite me to caress you. There is so much of you to see and to get to know. I see that you have bottled your estrogen pills to remind you of this changing time and have also bottled some of my baubles and sparkles to remember my spirit.

Youth Speaks To Gale:

Continue to enjoy me. Dress up, play, be social, flirt, dance, create and be spontaneous.

Age Speaks To Gale:

I'm so glad you appreciate all I have to offer. I bring depth to your experiences and to your creative efforts. Stay focused on the present, meditate, exercise, eat well and you will help me to grow stronger in mind and body. Be aware of artificial limitations. Look beyond.

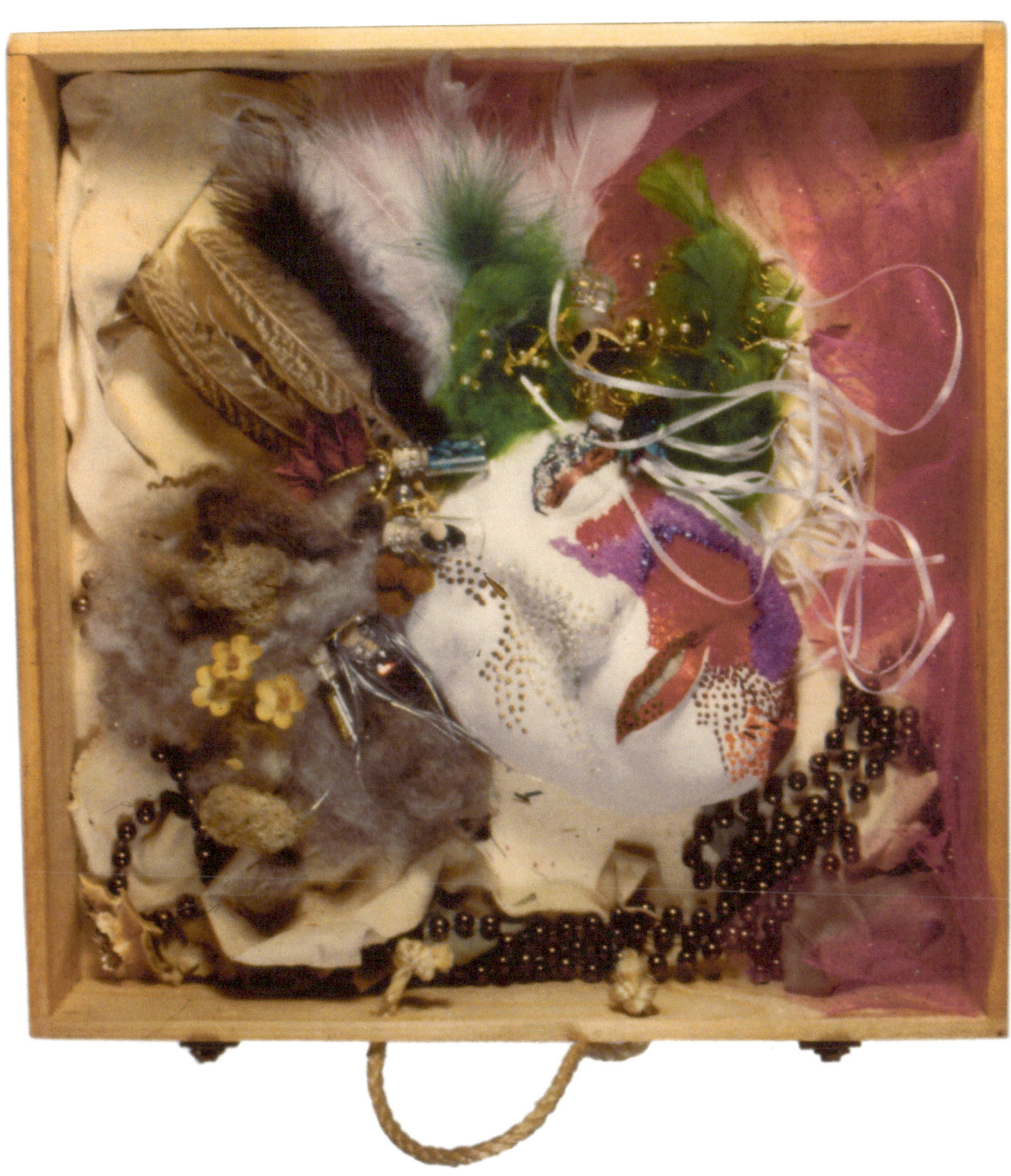

Recovering From Breast Cancer

I was dealing with a life-threatening illness having been diagnosed with breast cancer the previous year. I had come to realize the time and energy I had wasted over the years worrying about my body: shape, breasts, weight, hair, etc. I started a collage that clarified some of the socialization trends that make women so self-absorbed in their body image. This was a way for me to cast off some of these images and reaffirm what was most important for me now—my health. I felt safe in this workshop. I had warm feelings towards this group of women. Because of this, I wanted to express the feelings I had of caring, and sharing and a commonality of fear of breast cancer and other related female diseases. I created a circle of ribbon around the body image to signify the relatedness I had with these women. I used flowers to represent the beauty of this feeling of caring.

—Ilene, 40's

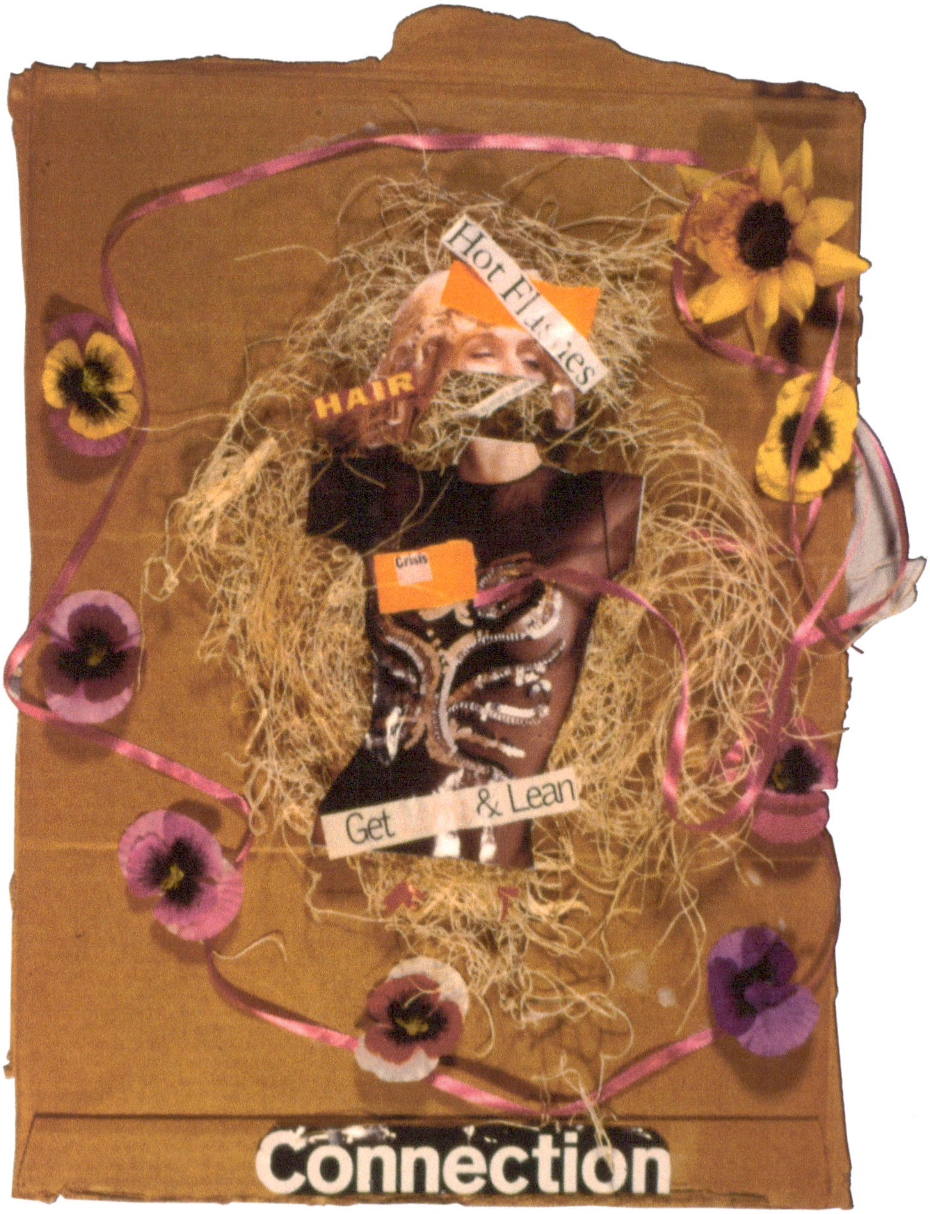

CHAPTER ELEVEN

A Room Of Your Own: Creating Personal Space

Building Boundaries With Collage Materials

If you have a sacred place and use it, take advantage of it, something will happen.

—Joseph Campbell

Claiming Your Corner

Creating a private, personal space for solitude, meditation, prayer, relaxation or journaling can be difficult in a crowded home. Constructing a "room" of your own can be as simple, however, as decorating a large piece of cardboard and using it to carve out or claim a corner of a larger room for quiet and reflective activities.

Creating Your Room

Many types of materials can be used to create your "room," including cardboard, wood, fencing, and wire which can be free-standing or placed against the wall. Cutting the ends and one side off of a tall cardboard box produces a three-sectioned surface which can form an enclosure around you. Four- and two-sectioned surfaces can be used as well. A three-sectioned presentation board can also be purchased from an office supply store.

Look for images and materials which are soothing and/or inspirational, then decorate your "room" in a way which is uniquely yours and fits your purpose. A three-sectioned surface can also serve as a vehicle for illustrating your life story; past, present, and a vision for your future. You can store your "room" and set it up whenever and wherever you want. Or leave it open in a corner of a room, to be available at all times for inspiration and seclusion.

We have used this concept with adults, as well as children as young as seven, working in children's groups at domestic violence service programs. The children have decorated multi-sectioned cardboard to form a colorful "safe space" around our group during our meetings. The children take their "safe space" home with them at the conclusion of group to remind them of what they've learned in the shelter program regarding self-care and safety.

You can also converse with your completed "room" and ask it how it wants to be decorated and how you can best put it to use.

Art is prayer… a fresh vital discovery of one's own special presence in the world.

–Joseph Zinker, Gestalt Psychotherapist

My Special Place

I wanted to work with a durable material, so I chose green fencing. Woven throughout is thick, beige lace. Attached with bead wire and silk ribbon, is all that visually pleases me, natural materials such as feathers, pearls, pinecones, wooden beads and bells. During meditation, I use my medicine animals, crystals, candles…. whatever is needed to enhance concentration and stimulate the magic of thought energy.

—Martha, 40's

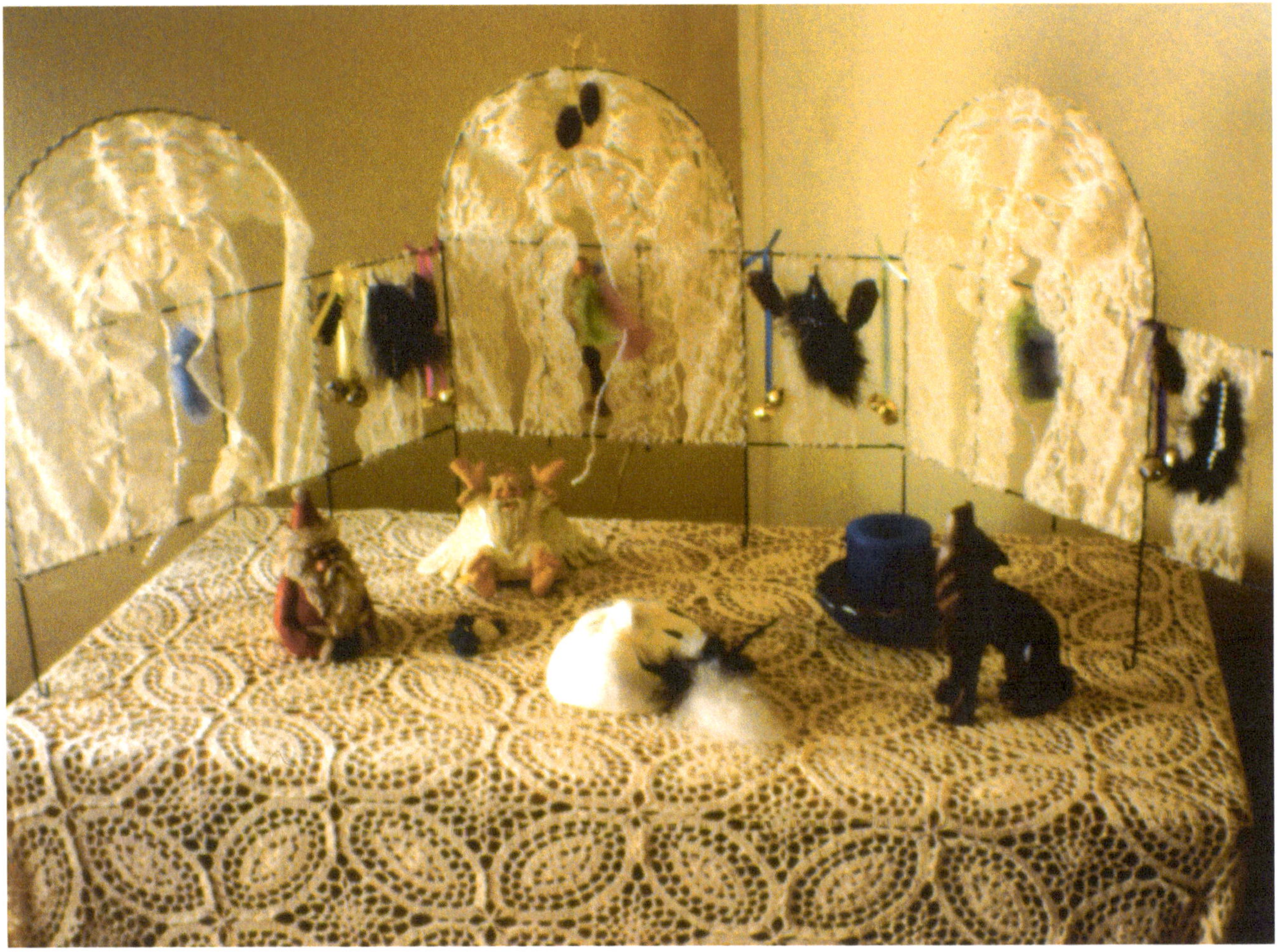

I Am Your Special Place.

Come to me when
You are lost and confused. Come to me when
You are angry and in pain.
I will help you find the answers you seek.
I am focus.

Emotions Deep In The Earth

My board is covered with colored tissue paper and starch to create a landscaped natural effect. The colors move from bright to earthy colors as my emotions moved from the surface to deeper, underneath the earth. The picture of the young woman is one I had been saving for several years, not knowing what I would use it for, pulling it out to use here. The owls are an image I also used in my fairy tale collage.

—Amanda, 20's

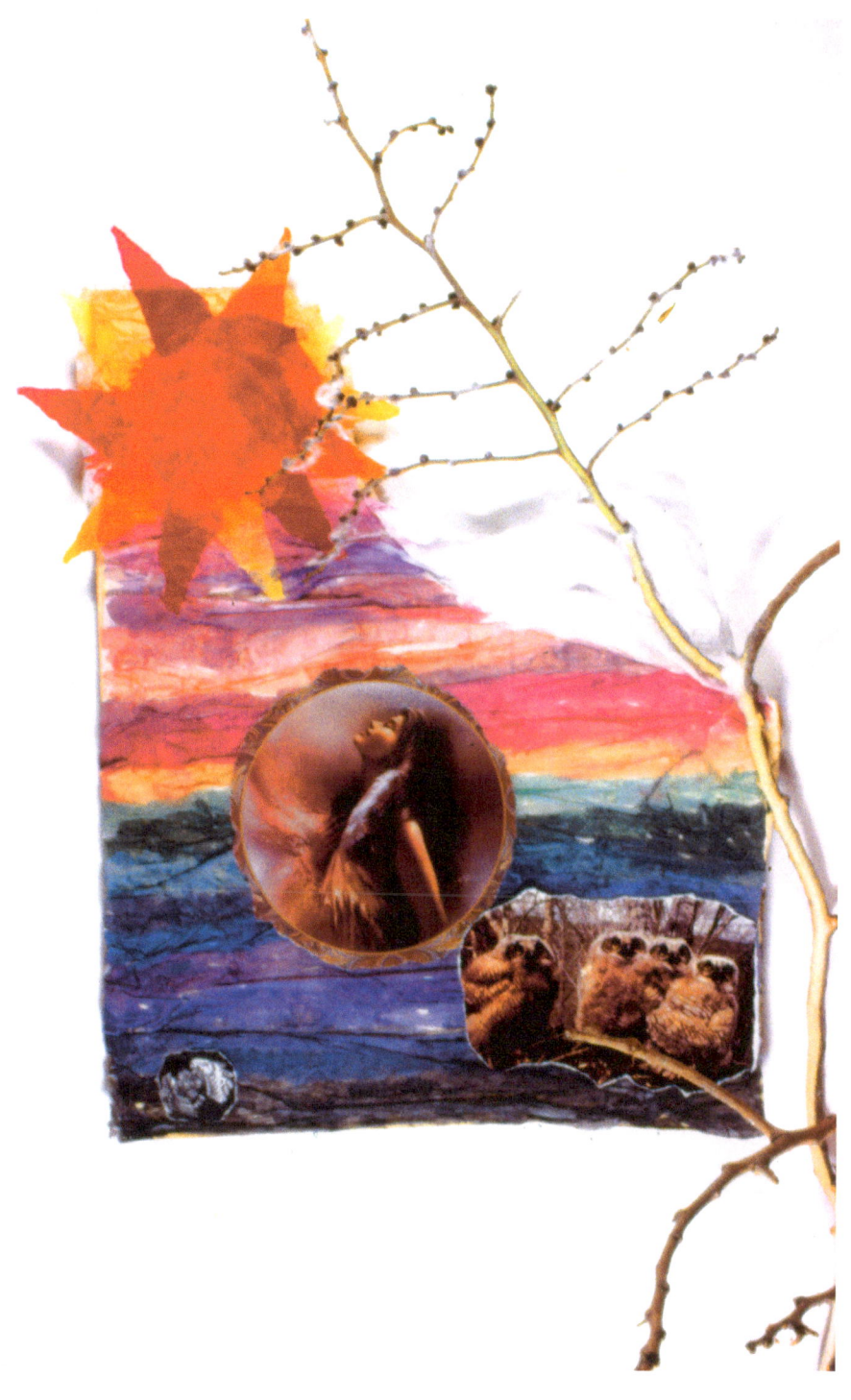

I Won't Hide From Myself Anymore

To my amazement, this project fell together so easily. It all started the Sunday after class when I found a board in a trash room at work. That night I started to look through magazines. One night after my husband and the dogs had gone to bed, I set up a circle with candles, lit some incense, made myself some sage tea and just relaxed for a few minutes before working on my meditation board.

I have always had an interest in animals and nature. During this class I have become interested in the use of candles to represent the four directions and the elements that are associated with each direction. In the past few years I have been learning about my totem animals. However, I have had trouble putting this information together, remembering it, applying it to my daily life, and using it. My board will be used as a tool to help me learn, meditate, find answers and understand questions about myself and my life.

I have placed all my totem animals in their correct directions, along with the season, element and time of day. Crow in the North; winter, earth, midnight (shown here). Lynx in the South; summer, fire, noon. Weasel in the East; spring, air, and sunrise. Dolphin in the West; fall, water and dusk. My Above animal is the Turtle (also shown here). My Below animal is the Moose, my Within animal is the Turkey, and to my right or male side is Dog and to my left or female side is Bear.

In the very center of my board is a framed mirror, and on the outside edges of this frame I had attached black feathers. To me, black is protection. The color black blends with everything, it does not stand out, and this is the way I like to be. However I have changed the color of the feathers to white. Although I am scared to death to stand out in a crowd, I do want to take steps not to hide from myself.

—Karen, 30's

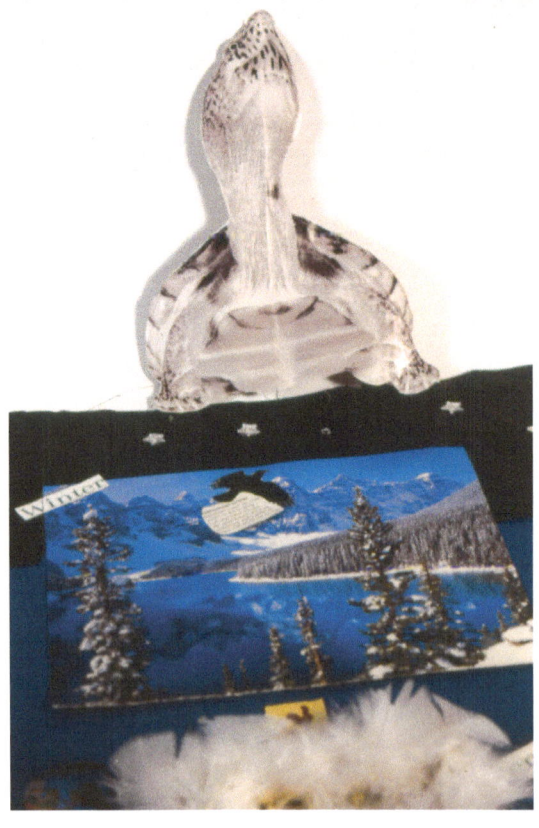

CHAPTER TWELVE

Making Your Dreams Reality

Visioning Your Hopes And Goals, And Moving Forward

*Every thought, every expectation—all of what we visualize happening
in the future—is a prayer and tends to create that very future.*

—James Redfield, author of
The Celestine Prophecy

Envision Your Goals

Constructing a detailed picture of what you want in your future will move you consistently forward toward your goal.

When you hold a clear picture of your goal, and something crosses your path that fits your picture, it will catch your attention, and you can incorporate it into your life.

Here Are Some Areas You May Wish To Consider When Setting Your Goals:

- Physical Health and Exercise
- Lifestyle/Possessions
- Money
- Community Involvement
- Spiritual Pursuits
- Relationships
- Leisure/Travel
- Education and Culture
- Work/Career
- Creative Self-Expression
- Emotional Well-Being
- Visions for the Planet

Collaging Your Goals

To begin, picture your goals and give yourself time to imagine them being accomplished. Then look for images which illustrate your goal in as much detail as possible. Don't give up if you do not see a clear picture. Merely starting this process can help you to clarify the details. You can add new images to your collage whenever you find them, as they may not all come to you at once.

After completing your collage, converse with it and ask it what you need to do first. Let each image talk about itself. Taking your first steps toward a goal can be difficult, but once you take these steps you will build forward momentum. Continue to check in with your collage to find out what the next steps are.

Post your collage where you can see it frequently and look it over from time to time. This will keep you on track and remind you of your commitment.

Families, couples, groups of friends, neighbors, work groups, and community groups can use this process to envision and achieve desired goals.

*When I look into the future it's so
bright it burns my eyes.*

—Oprah Winfrey

At The Heart Of Wellness

This collage is a visual reminder of the week-ly activities which help me to stay healthy and which keep me in good spirits. The images raise my enthusiasm every time I look at them. At the heart of my wellness plan is my med-itation practice. When I remember to honor my inner child through singing and laughter, I'm a "happy camper"! I eat a lot of healthy foods, but I'm not a purist, and I've tucked a piece of pie behind my glass of carrot juice. My bedtime reading (tucked behind Echinacea flower) is *Don't Sweat the Small Stuff*. Journaling and art making are essential to my soul.

—Ginny, 50's

Heart Speaks To Ginny:

Lead with your heart and you will never go wrong. I resonate with all the walking you're doing!

Third Eye (On Forehead Of Meditating Figure) Speaks To Ginny:

Don't forget me. My intuition can help your heart to "see" clearly.

Inner Child Speaks To Ginny:

Lighten up! You take things too seriously. Where's your sense of humor?

Turtle Speaks To Ginny:

Follow the Buddha's advice: "There is much to be done; Therefore, we must proceed slowly."

Painter Speaks To Ginny:

Well, I'm still waiting for you to get back to me. As soon as this book is finished, pick up your paints. You'll be sorry later if you neglect me.

Sleeper Speaks To Ginny:

This late night stuff isn't doing you any good. Take care of your sleep needs and everything else gets taken care of. No kidding!

Women Speak To Ginny:

Women working together can heal this world. Don't underestimate your power to create exactly what you want.

Carrot Juice Speaks To Ginny:

Enjoy me and you can enjoy your carrot cake, too! Variety is still the spice of life!

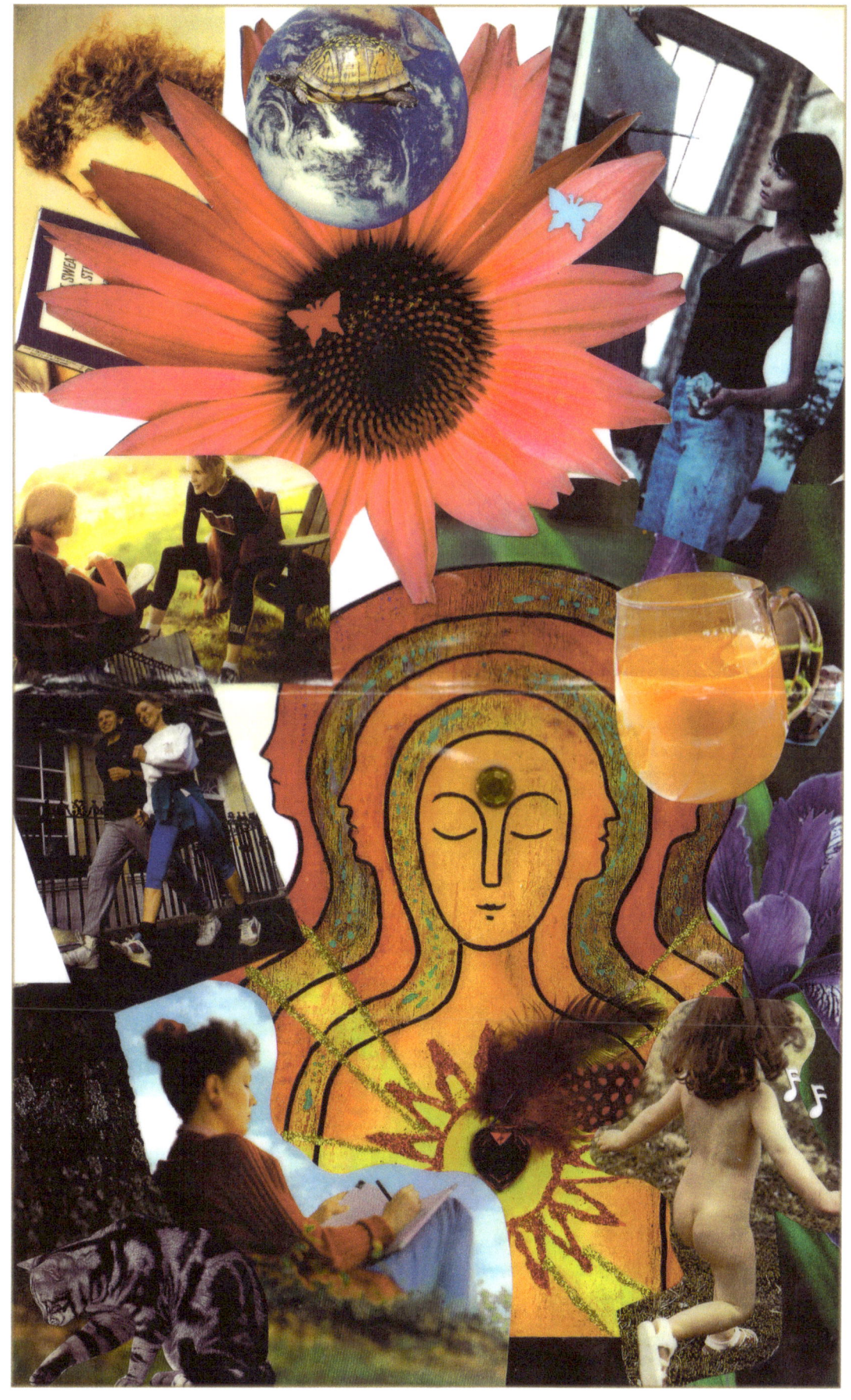

Taking Time For Spirit

This is a nametag I made for a workshop on spirituality and expressive art.

I strive to stay on a spiritual path and these images help to remind me of the things I need to keep in my life.

—Gale, 60's

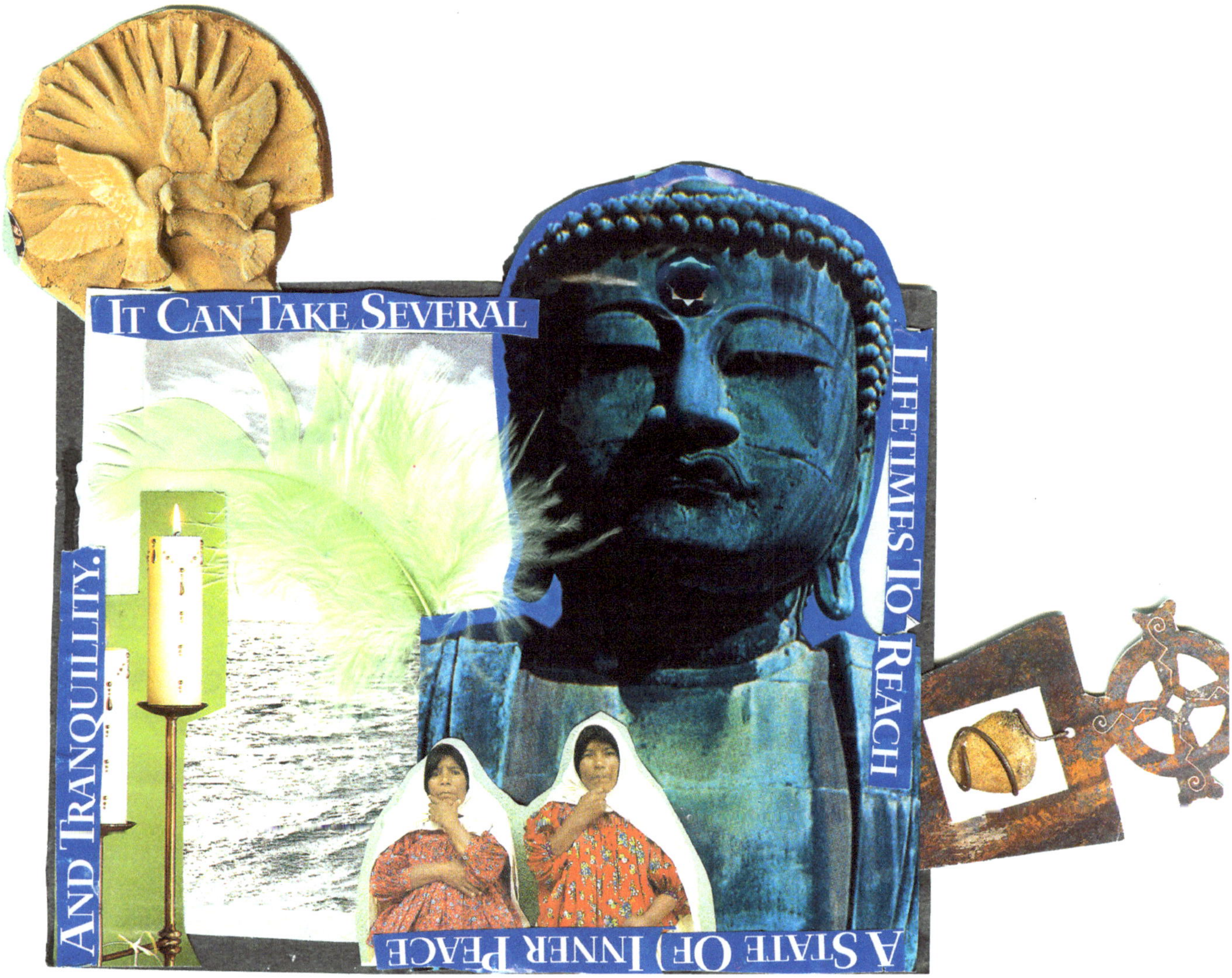

Buddha Speaks:

Set time aside, ready your space. Surround yourself with representatives of the four directions, earth, air, fire and water. Wait, keep waiting, sit, wait, sit, sit, stop waiting. Expect nothing. I may join you.

CHAPTER THIRTEEN

Your Collage Journal:
A Record Of Life's Journey In Images

We feed our imaginations and get in touch with our authenticity
by gathering together beautiful images that speak to our souls....
Meditating on one visual image a day can jump-start
your creativity and lead to revealing insights.

—*Sarah Ban Breathnach, author of* Simple Abundance

Your Journey In Images

Journaling is a process of recording your thoughts on a regular basis over a period of time. It can serve as a record of your personal development or for the exploration of a theme. It can also provide a daily discipline to keep ideas and creativity flowing.

A collage journal is a collection of collages glued to the blank pages of a sketch book or journal. Simple images can express complex thoughts with the additional enjoyment of visual stimulation. It is often said that one picture is worth a thousand words. This style of journaling is especially helpful to those who find words restrictive or cumbersome at this particular time in their lives. Many people who have given up traditional journaling techniques have reported renewed interest and deeper expression by using images to symbolize concepts, experiences, and emotions. Traditional journaling can be combined with collage journaling if space is allowed to converse with the images or make personal notes and comments, or add a quote or poem. A collage journal becomes your autobiography in images.

Your collage journal can express how you are feeling today or explore other subjects of interest such as wellness, gratitude, forgiveness, and comfort. We have discovered that the longer we practice,

the more we feel free to experiment with new ways of using collage in our journals. Sometimes we explore a particular theme for a while, and then switch to another. Sometimes we work with complex images, then experiment with simplicity. Sometimes we like to use single images which take up a whole page. We create three-dimensional pages in pop-up formats, cut see-through pages and occasionally have the images flow from one page to the next. The journal has become a vehicle for exploring the expressive arts process as well as a chosen theme.

You can use your journal to collect images, poems, quotes, stories and other writings, which provide constant inspiration and can be revisited especially when your spirits are low. Feel free to collect images that appeal to you and paste them in your journal and do nothing with them at all other than look at them. One collage journalist creates visual prayers in her prayer journal for both personal and global issues.

At times you may be disappointed with the outcome of a collage. Making a decision about what to do about it is a worthy exploration in itself. Do you simply rip it out, cover it up, change it, or work to accept it as it is? What can you learn from observing your reaction to disappointment? Is that how

(Continued on p. 102)

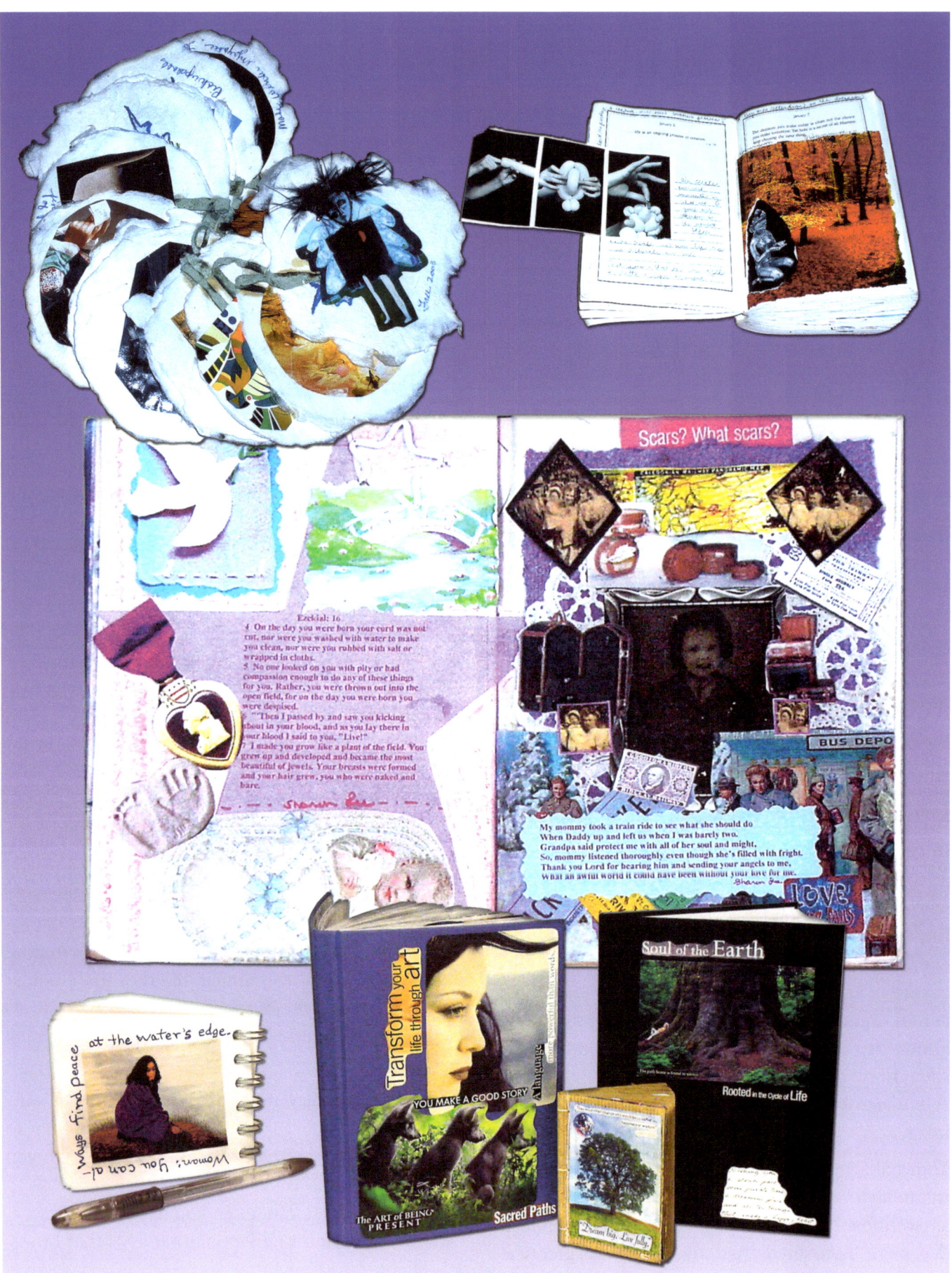

Butterfly At Daybreak

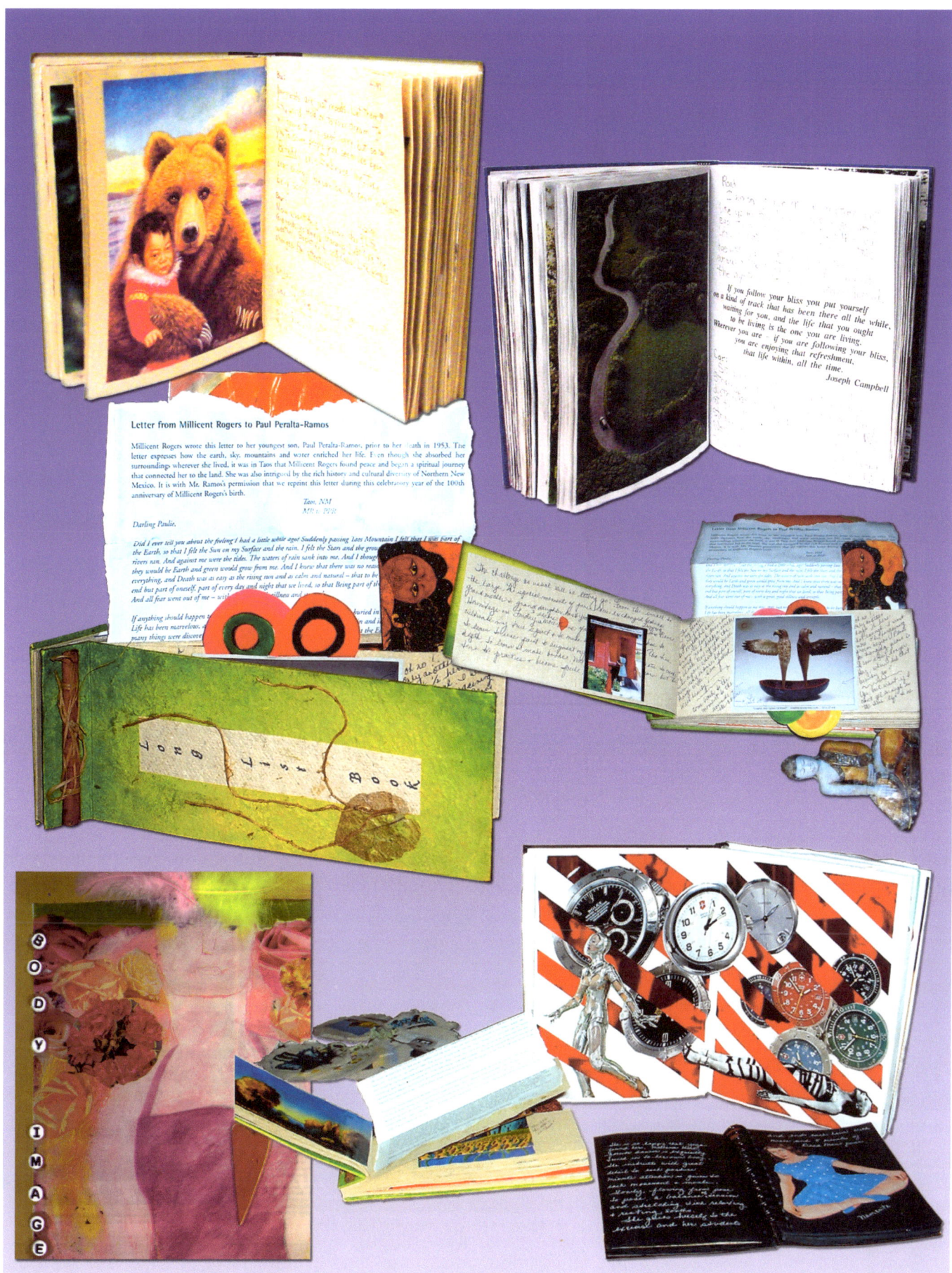

you operate in everyday life when you are not happy with the outcome of a project?

Does this teach you anything about how you tend to react to disappointing aspects of yourself?

Collage journals come in many sizes and shapes with a variety of bindings and can even be hand-made by the journal keeper. A smaller journal is more easily portable and can be carried while traveling, along with a small scissors and bottle of glue. Journals can incorporate feathers, sequins, glitter, ribbons, and colored tissue paper as well as more traditional materials like charcoal and paint. Scrapbooking materials and techniques can also be incorporated. Your journal cover can be decorated with collage and craft items too. And you can work in several journals at once. Remember, anything goes. Each sitting can be completely different. Experiment with what works for you and be prepared to change course as your needs change.

A Letter From Your Journal

Before you begin a new journal, you might converse with it. Ask your new, blank journal what it wants from you or how it would like to be used. You might want to place this "letter" from your journal on the front page of your new journal.

It isn't necessary to work in your journal every day. Sometimes issues are clarified and wonderful shifts take place during the times you are not creating daily images. Trust yourself to know when you need to take a break from your journaling process. You will find yourself coming back to it when the time is right.

A Collage Journal Can Be Used To Document Your Life Day-by-Day Or Can Focus On Specific Themes, Such As:

- Prayer
- Recovery from grief
- Journey through hard times

- Wellness journey
- Visions for the future
- History of childhood
- Life review

- Gratitude
- Comfort and inspiration
- Spiritual journey

Look for your journals and unlined sketchbooks at bookstores and art supply stores. Purchase an easel/book stand at an art supply store to prop up and display your journal to view your favorite pages.

In many other cultures, it is commonplace to retreat from everyday life for a prescribed time and get in touch with that aspect of ourselves that is not goal-directed and time-oriented, is not concerned with gaining and losing but is boundless and infinite. I call this aspect The One Who is Not Busy.

—Darlene Cohen,
Finding a Joyful Life in a Heart of Pain

CHAPTER FOURTEEN

One Woman's Journey

Negotiating A Medical Crisis

When you have quieted your mind enough and transcended your ego enough you can hear how it really is.

—Baba Ram Dass

I remember feeling a strong need to find relief from my growing nervousness after I had a suspicious mammogram the last week in December 2001. There were more films taken, then a biopsy and then the dreaded diagnosis, Breast Cancer. Not long after, I had the pre-surgery needle placement and then the lumpectomy, followed by the tissue healing process and plans for the follow-up treatment.

At times I found myself at "loose ends." That was about as close as I could come to describing what I was feeling. I was unsettled and stuck with a great buzz of anxiety lurking. It was difficult to tease apart all the aspects of what was going on inside. I was unable to catch hold of my courage and my faith that all would be okay, whatever the outcome.

For a month and a half I chronicled this medical journey whenever I felt the need. I cut out magazine pictures that captured my roller coaster emotions.

I had each image speak about its purpose and meaning and then speak to me. Each time I completed a collage, I would thaw out a little more, becoming more aware of what was going on inside of me and more in control of my thinking.

By embodying my fear and various other feelings with concrete images and giving them a voice, they could have their full-bodied say and move on. My fears diminished, no longer running my life, and my faith grew. It is always essential for me to give my fears and uncomfortable feelings their say as well as hearing from my more upbeat feelings.

Even with the wonderful support of friends and family, a serious health problem or any problem causing great concern can make for lonely moments. You're still faced with going through this, like it or not. It took courage to make room for solitude and it took solitude to remember my inner strength. Befriending myself by going deep inside, by making collages, was a comforting, bolstering, transformative experience for me. The following are a few of the collages I made during that time.

Gale, 60's

What a gift of grace to be able to take the chaos from within and from it create some semblance of order.

—Katherine Paterson

Man With The Horn

Optical Illusion Band:

I am the illusive wall that keeps you from intense fear. I am not strong enough to do the job on my own well enough. Intense fear rushes past me and gets to your calmer, functional parts. When you keep busy, talk to people, do everyday chores, you are helping me to do my job of keeping us apart from the wild horses and the flames. Going to the health club for exercise, taking a walk would probably help strengthen me.

Man With The Horn:

HEAR YE, HEAR YE! YOU ARE IN BIG FUCKING TROUBLE. THE BIG CANCER. IT'S GOING TO BE BAD NEWS. THE BIOPSY WILL BE DONE POORLY. RESULTS WILL BE INCORRECT. ANY WAY YOU CUT IT IT'S CANCER, NON-TREATABLE CANCER, NON-RESPONSIVE CANCER. NO LUMPECTOMY, RADIATION, TAMOXIFEN FOR YOU! MASTECTOMY AND CHEMO FOR YOU! HAIR LOSS AND UGLY WIG FOR YOU! DEATH AND SUFFERING IS IMMINENT.

What's my purpose here? Ah… I think I am helping you to prepare for the worst. Not to be caught off guard. To make you realize the dangers, to help you to be prepared.

Gale To Man:

But look what you are doing here to the horses. Can that be good for them/us? They are completely out of control. Tremendous power, out of control. Undirected, stampeding, of danger to themselves and others. How can I get you to help me prepare without the stampede?

Man:

Get a clearer picture of the unseen voice of faith. You have it, feel it for others. How come not yourself?

Gale To Man:

When I have it for others, you, little horn man, are not blasting me with the worst possible outcomes. I will consider getting a clearer picture of faith. Maybe Ram Dass or Deepak will help.

Invisible Voice (not pictured):

You will be okay. You will be scared but you will be all right no matter what. I am your faith, I think. Place yourself in my hands, turn your fears over to me. We, together, will do what needs to be done. That's all that is essential now. Staying in the moment and doing what needs to be done. Place the burden in my hands. I will help you take the necessary actions. Staying in the moment with an action plan is the right action. I need you to use your energy for the action plan. Read the material, consider a second opinion at Northwestern Hospital. Ask questions about both breasts. Make a collage to represent me, your faith.

I am functional. I can carry your burdens of fear. The little man with the horn is frightened. When you put him in my arms he relaxes.

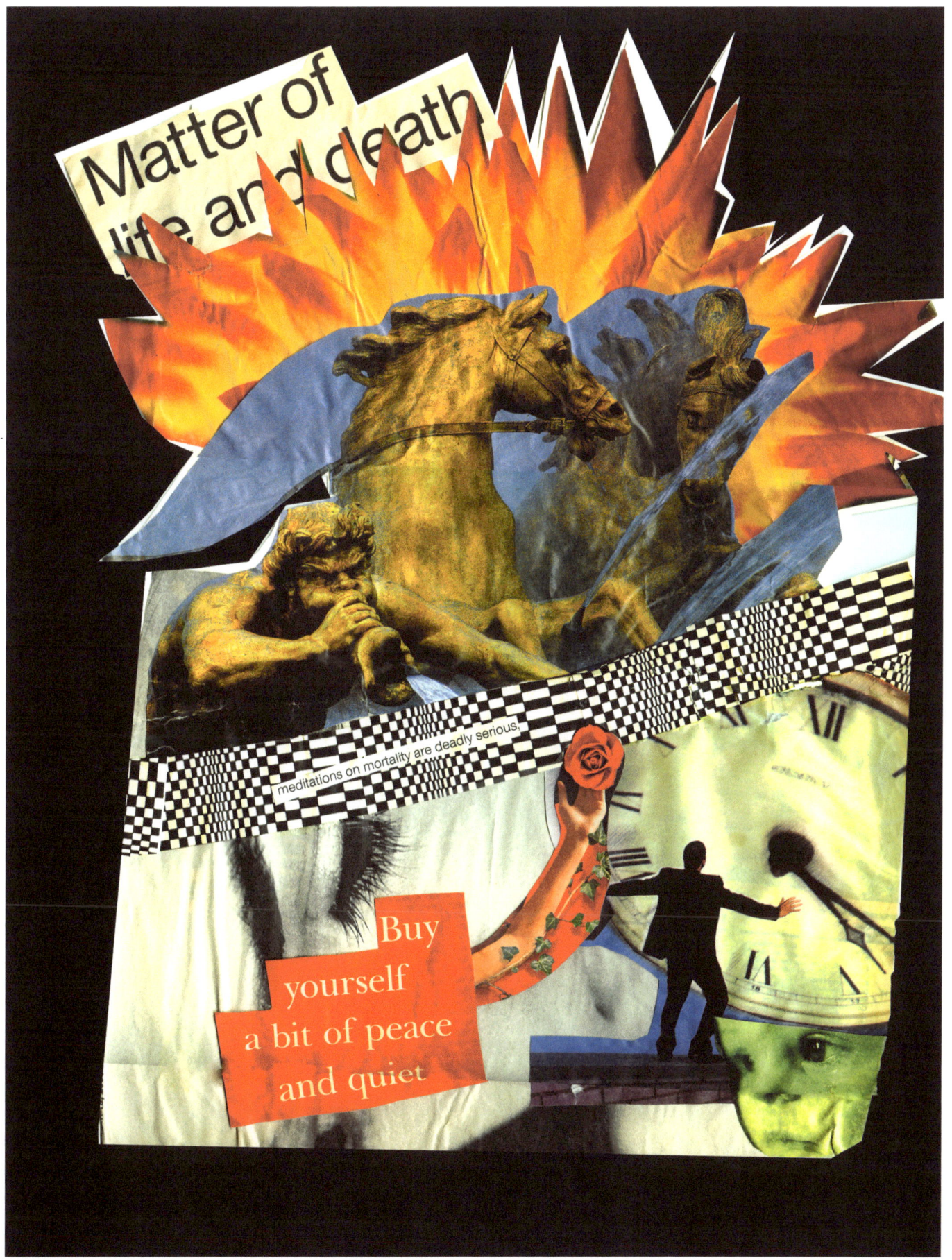

The Presence Of Love

January 10, 2001

(Night before results of biopsy)

Manatee:

I am the voice of goodness and peace and love. I am with you. Tonight I am in your forefront. I cover you like a warm blanket. Underneath though, there are rumblings of anxiety. I will do my best to remain in your forefront.

Stranger:

I lurk here behind the tree trunk, partially hidden. I am here to scare you. I am the boogie man. Actually, I mean you no harm. I appear when you scare yourself about the future. Let me remind you to stay in the present. You will deal with what is necessary as the time comes. You have all the support you need.

The Crow:

I am almost free. Partly free. I scare you, too. I am of blood. You do not know me. I do not know me.

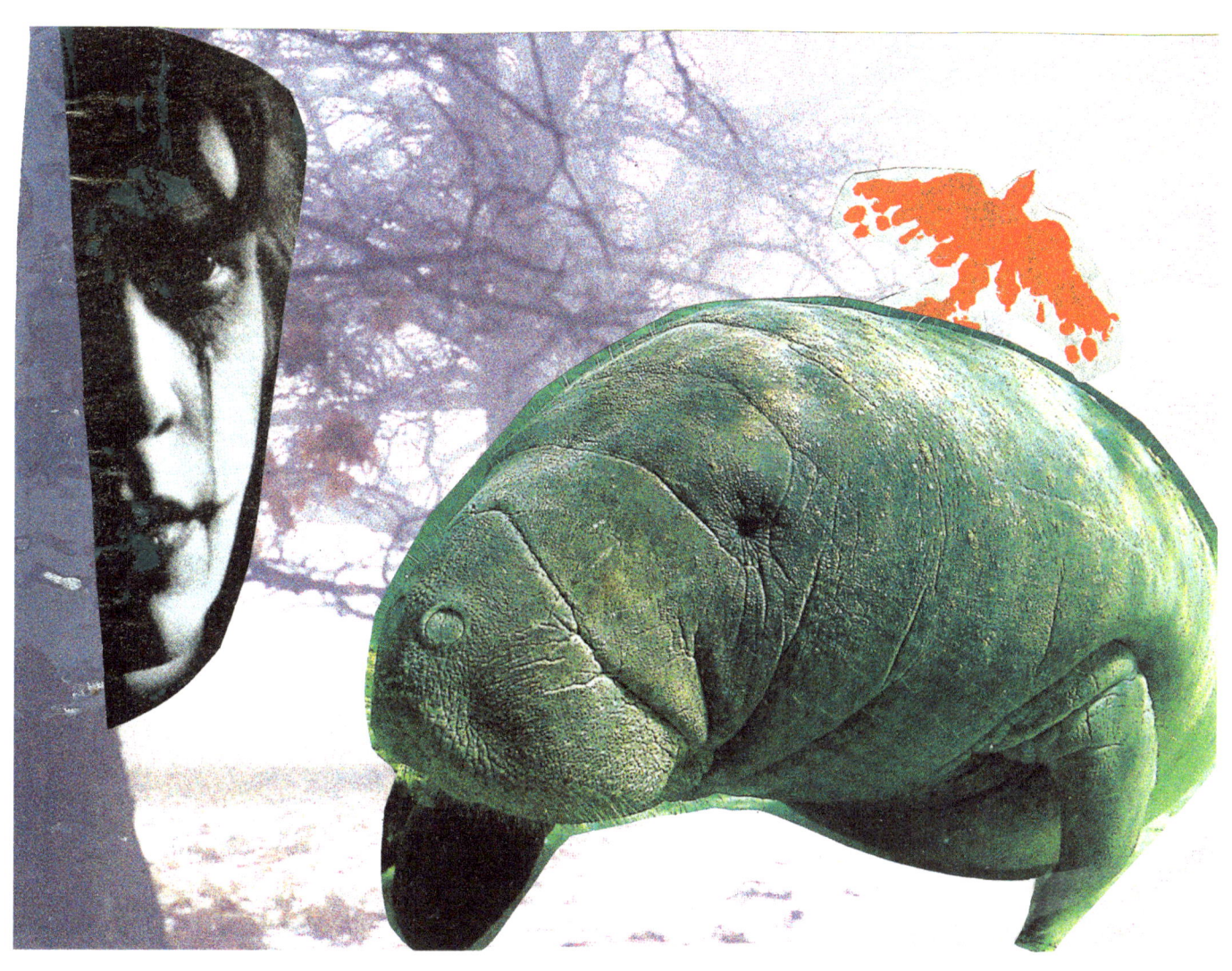

Awaiting News

January 11, 2001

Front Page: (see below)

Still innocent, unknowing, frightened beneath the surface.

Inner Page, After The Phone Call With The Cancer Diagnosis:
(see opposite page)

Woman:

*The best of the worst, the nurse said, "Cancer at a very early stage." Sadness. Just sadness.
Sadness I've been anticipating for a long time I think. A beginning too. Of what, I do not know.*

Gale:

I give thanks to all the women friends who have gone through this before with courage
and good humor. They give me courage. Especially thanks to Ilene and Nancy.

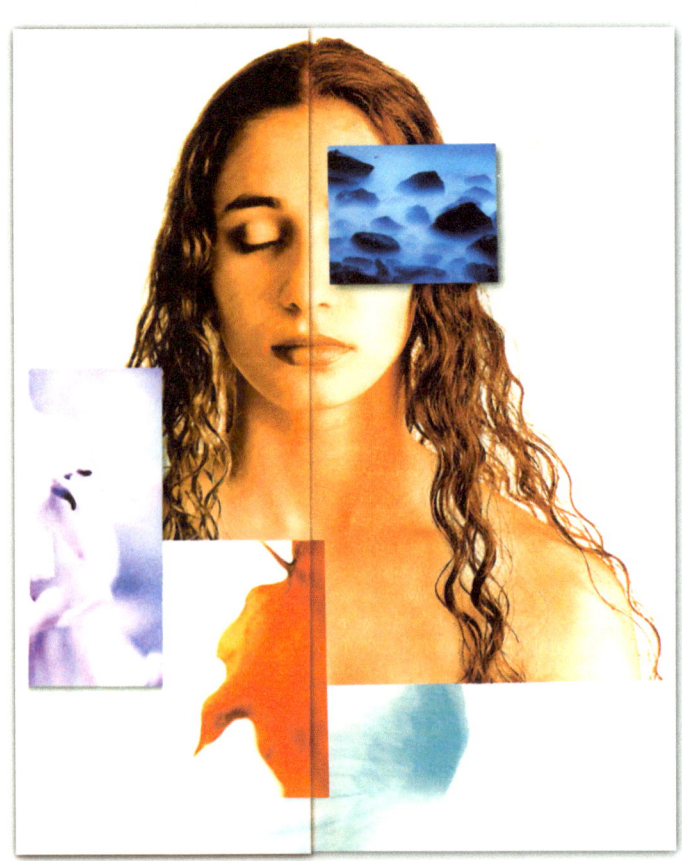

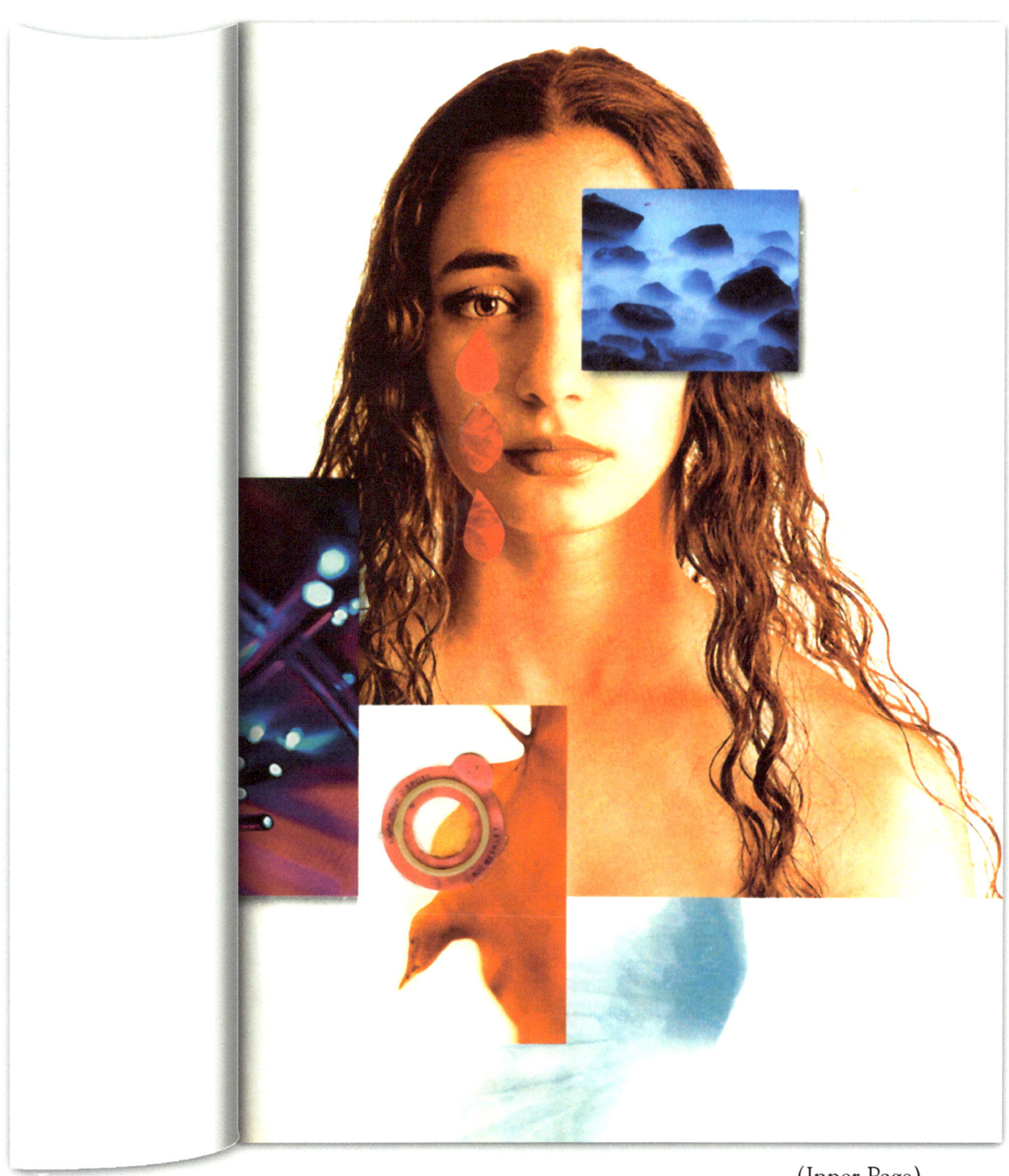

(Inner Page)

Goddess Band-Aid

January 18, 2001

(After a phone call from the hospital telling me of heart irregularities picked up in the pre-op EKG)

Gale To Heart:

I am so sad about your problems. I feel so helpless. Your problems add complications to my other health issues. I do not want to be afraid of you. You are so important to me physically and seem to be the place in my body that experiences so many of my emotions. The very best of them and the worst of them. I will take care of you the best I can.

Heart To Gale:

I may have more to say later. Right now I say, I am what I am and have always been so all these almost 62 years. Like the plumber said, pipes and tubes and faucets and valves wear with age. I have been well used, actively used and have wear and tear. It can't be helped. Find out more about what you can do to help to keep me strong and healthy. Remember though that you can only do so much. Appreciate the efforts you have already made, soy, exercise, low fat food. Now work on the emotional relaxing. Reduce the ever present pressure of not having enough time. Clarify priorities. This arena needs work. Get your affairs in order in case I go off the deep end. Remember to enjoy each day. Keep focused on love and gratitude. Set limits on what stressors to deal with and which ones to let go.

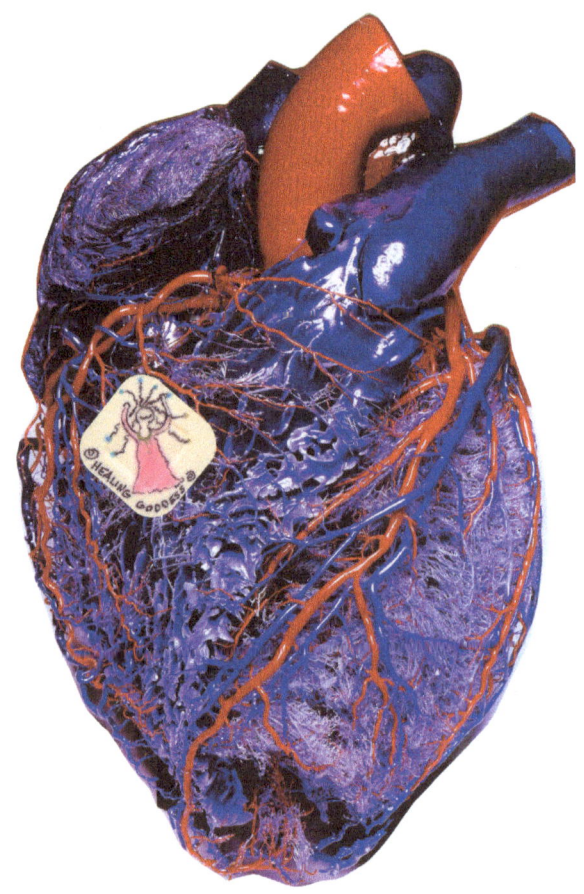

Woman Spirit

January 22, 2001

(Two days prior to surgery)

Pillar Speaks:

I am so complex, so rich, so versatile and beautiful. I am absolutely non-uniform and unpredictable. I am magical. I am you and much more than you have dared to be. I am the Goddess and I have sent you out to find out all about yourself. You are beautiful, interesting, colorful and more. It will take a lot longer to know this much about yourself. I wish you many years to do this.

Woman Speaks:

My breasts are so prominent and beautiful. So colorful, so feminine. Unfortunately they carry danger too. May I place myself in your hands? To let go of fear, to dare to do more? To be all that I can be?

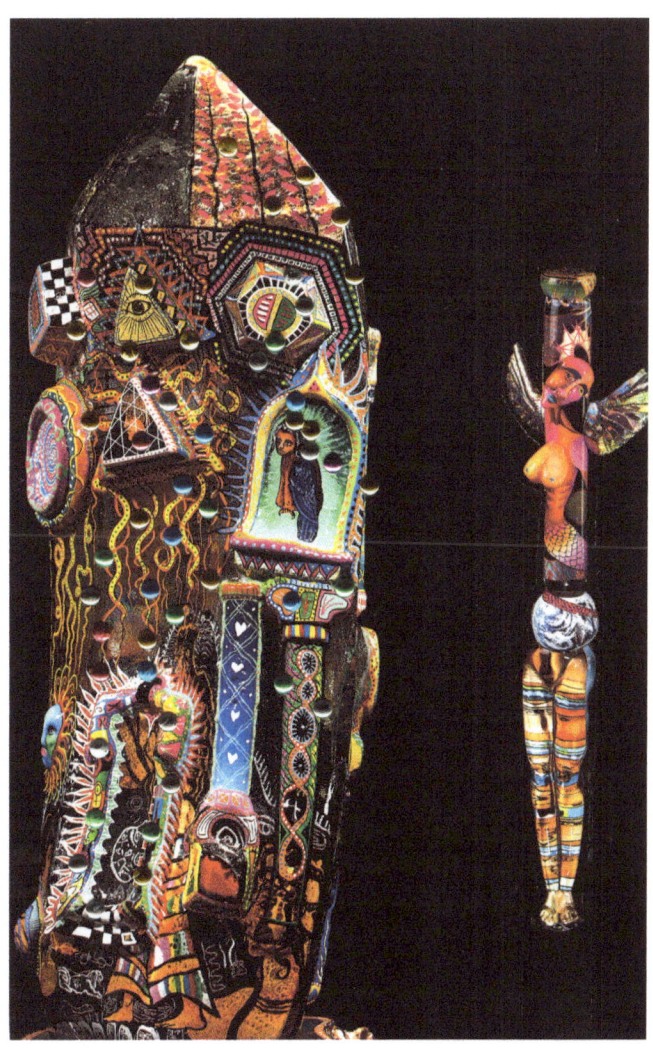

Baby Talk

January 29, 2001

*Five days after the lumpectomy, I dreamt about a baby I was caring for.
I had forgotten about her and had been negligent and the possible consequences were serious.*

Baby Speaks:

Don't let me down. I am very much present in your unconscious. I am vulnerable now. You have never proven to me that you can care for babies or animals with enough attention. Are you thinking that life will go on as usual with no side effects? Yes, you were thinking that. Isn't that a bit unrealistic?

Gale Speaks:

I do the best I can.

Breast Speaks:

What is going on here? I am hard and painful and inflamed and you two are talking about old business. Make me your concern today. I am putting Gale on edge. Be patient.

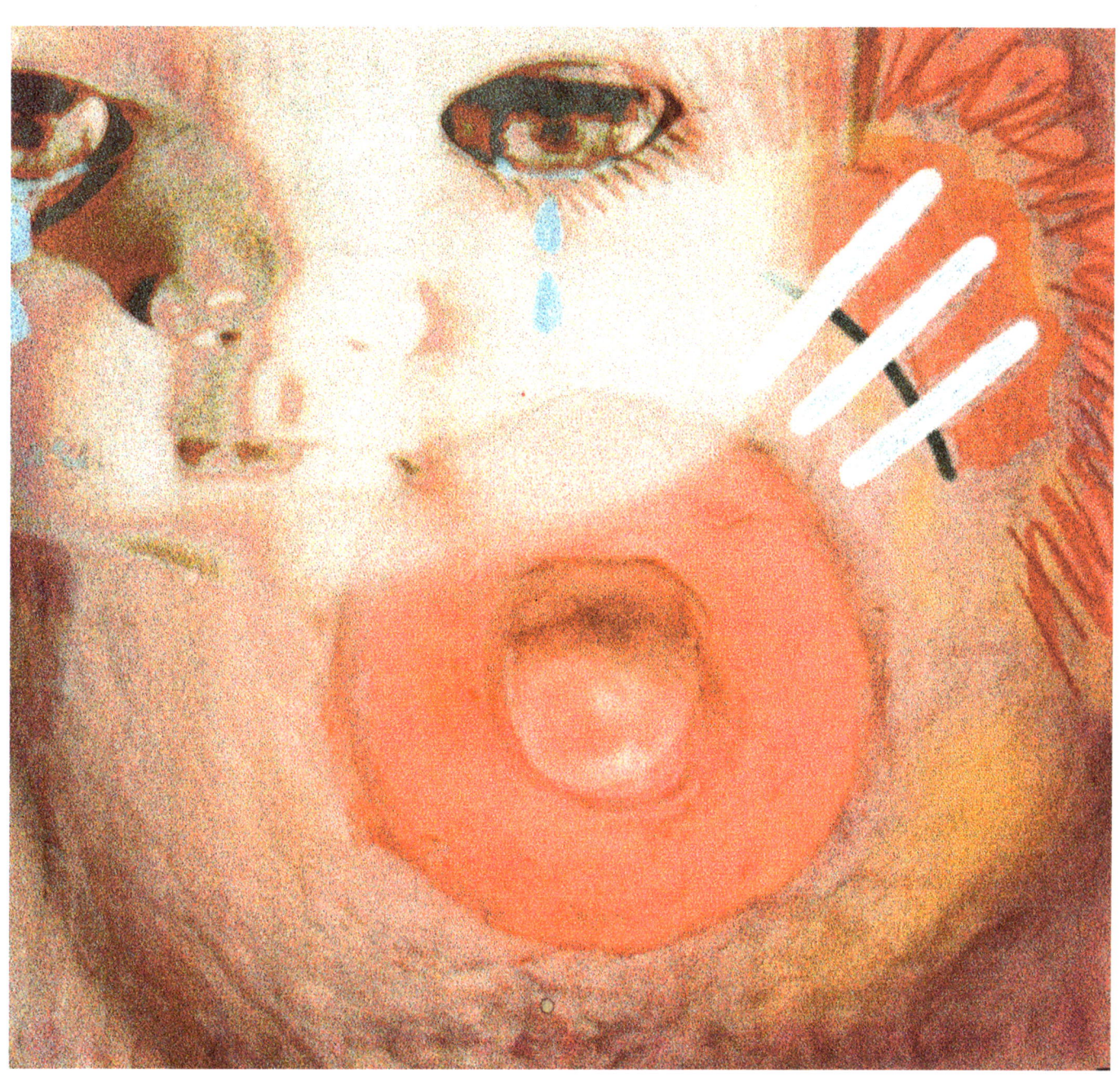

Valentine's Day On Maui

February 14, 2001

This collage was a last look at the feelings during the medical crisis. Four "second" opinions quoted a 98 percent chance of complete recovery due to early diagnosis.

Still, having cancer or any other life-threatening illness is life changing and the thoughts and feelings arising from this are unfolding gradually. I am on the threshold of new musings.

I was grateful to be able to follow the January of intense self-focus with a trip to Hawaii. It was a breath of fresh air and provided a necessary change of scene. How helpful that can be.

My personal use of collage through the crisis strengthened my belief in this amazing process. It is so simple to do and basically requires so few materials. For this series, I only used magazines, glue and scissors. (oh yes, a bit of glitter too)

Puppy Speaks:

I represent your most loving attachment feelings; for your little granddaughter Iris at this moment who you so long to see and hold. Your sadness for little Wadley dog, killed so recently by a car. I am definitely a pressure in your life right now. I need attention.

Pele Goddess Of The Volcano Speaks:

I hold you in my arms. I offer you comfort and care. I am with you. I bring you the best I have to give. You in turn must take good care of your body. Remember me. Think of the mist of rain that fell when you called out to me in the "devil's garden" lava field.

Solitude Speaks:

Just a brief time alone can be healing. Find a balance.

Pills Speak:

We are your underlying fears of the future. The worst of what can be ahead. I grow in size if you ignore me. Actually I covered the page until Gale decided to only use a corner of my original size in an effort to reduce my negativity.

Bronze Statue Speaks:

I represent Ilene. Little sister, also a lost innocent doing the best she can with her breast cancer and some of the same fears. May she also be protected and comforted by Pele.

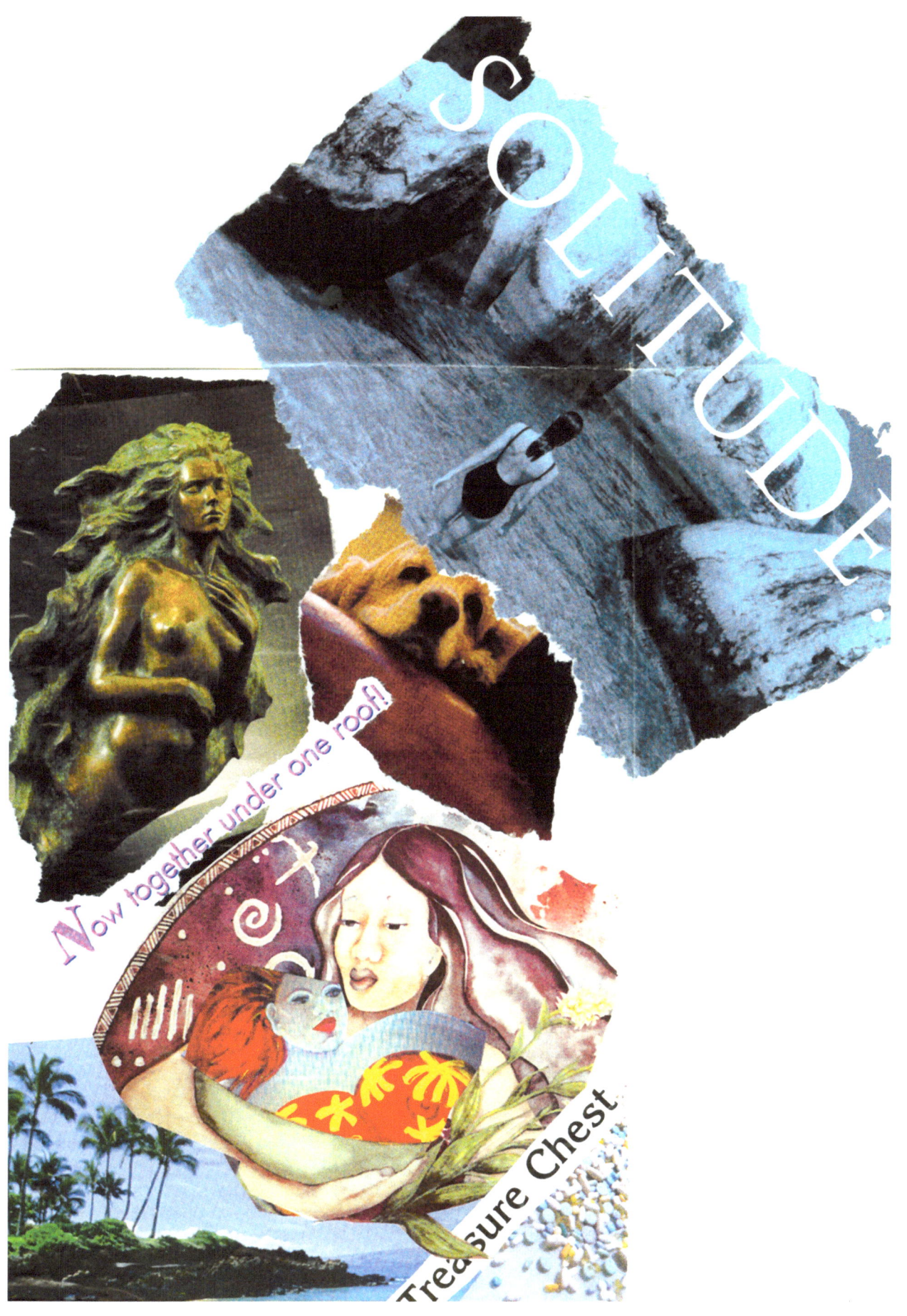

SOLITUDE.

Now together under one roof!

Treasure Chest

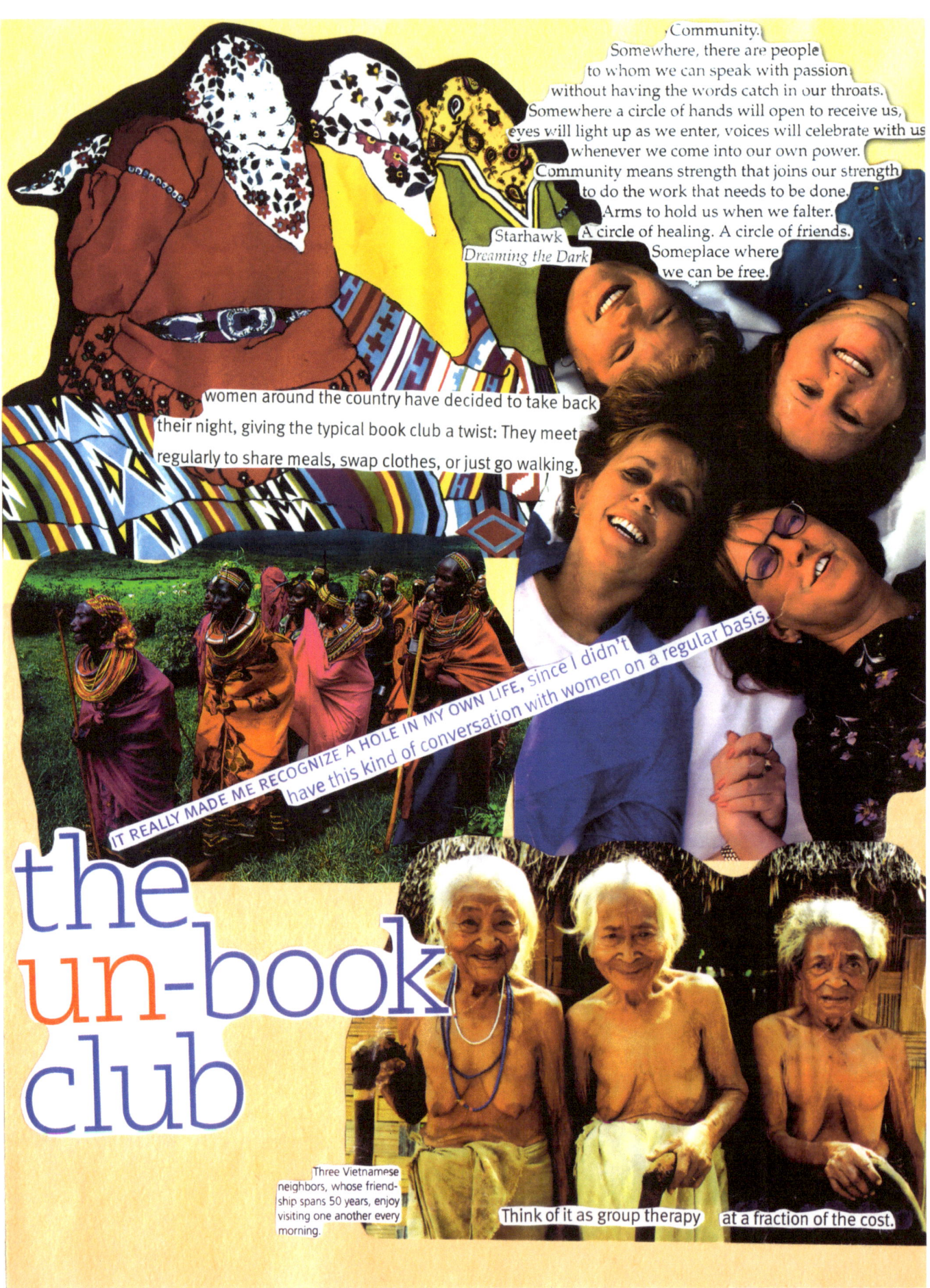

Community.
Somewhere, there are people
to whom we can speak with passion
without having the words catch in our throats.
Somewhere a circle of hands will open to receive us,
eyes will light up as we enter, voices will celebrate with us
whenever we come into our own power.
Community means strength that joins our strength
to do the work that needs to be done.
Arms to hold us when we falter.
A circle of healing. A circle of friends.
Someplace where
we can be free.

Starhawk
Dreaming the Dark

women around the country have decided to take back
their night, giving the typical book club a twist: They meet
regularly to share meals, swap clothes, or just go walking.

IT REALLY MADE ME RECOGNIZE A HOLE IN MY OWN LIFE, since I didn't
have this kind of conversation with women on a regular basis.

the un-book club

Three Vietnamese
neighbors, whose friend-
ship spans 50 years, enjoy
visiting one another every
morning.

Think of it as group therapy   at a fraction of the cost.

APPENDIX A

Forming An Expressive Arts Group For You And Your Friends

Entrance to another's soul is always a sacred honor.

—J. Stone, Stone Cards

Sharing Collages

Sharing the expressive arts experience with friends in a group setting has many benefits. Seeing each other's collages gives you ideas about using collage materials in new ways. Often group members are exploring similar issues and as you listen to a friend talk about her collage, you develop new insights into your own situation. For example, one of our group members made 10 color copies of an image related to body size. She asked the group if we would all be interested in using it as the starting point for our collage that day. It was interesting to see how each person's collage could be so unique and yet constructed around an identical image.

Sometimes you may see yourself so clearly in someone else's collage that it seems as if that person made the collage just for you. And sometimes group members can see something in your collage that you didn't see until they pointed it out. When you share your work with others, you feel seen and heard in a healthy way. A group experience can feel very rich.

Putting A Group Together

There are many ways you can organize your collage group. You can invite friends to join you once or twice a month. We had a group of about 15 friends

join us twice a month to make collages. Not everyone decided to come back after the first meeting and a few have dropped out over time. We have invited a few new members since we began. Attendance at every session is not required. Some attend almost every session, while others tend to come and go. We have about 4-8 friends in attendance every time we meet. This has worked for us; another arrangement might work for you. You may not feel focused or disciplined enough to schedule collage making into your busy life. Working with a group can guarantee your success at doing collage at regular intervals.

Doing Group Work

To start, someone shares a quote or a poem, or we ring a set of chimes to focus our attention on being present. We spend a few minutes of quiet time. Then we work individually on our collages for about an hour and a half, each of us choosing a subject of our own personal interest. We usually have soft music playing in the background. At a predetermined time we gather back in a circle and take turns sharing our collages. You can choose to share as much of your collage as you wish. A timekeeper makes sure that the time spent sharing is evenly divided. If a group member has some of her allotted time left after sharing her collage, group members are invited to share observations or ask questions about the collage. Be aware that what is shared by other members of the group is confidential.

Remember this is not a time to criticize or interpret another person's work or to give advice about a problem. We simply talk about what we notice.

Also, remember that collage is not created as art or decoration, so try to refrain from commenting on the beauty of individual collages.

On a practical note, we have experimented with collecting $5 per person for a few months, then spending the money to purchase our supplies.

Some of our money went toward purchasing unusual magazines which could be found at larger or specialty book stores and provided some really striking and unusual images.

Every time I join the circle, during the beginning quiet time, I feel the tears slide down on my cheeks. I know it is about reconnecting to a part of me that I often leave behind… as I run around in my busyness. A small voice inside me cries… Where have you been? I need you!

—Deb Beaty

I open my just finished meditating eyes
And see my Artmates.
How precious they are to me.

Quietly busy, cutting and rustling,
Heartfully captivated, silently animated,
Absorbed, in action,
Eyes flitting, deft of hand,
Engaged, eager,
Intuitively jostling papers, deeply engrossed,
Listening to an inner knowing,
Moving about,
Everything new, original,
Pulsing with life,
Open to seeing in different ways,
Sorting and pasting,
Tying up loose ends,
Viewing, waiting,
Excited "yes" women, fully in the moment.

And now we share.

—Gale wrote this during our collage group meeting, describing the activity around her.

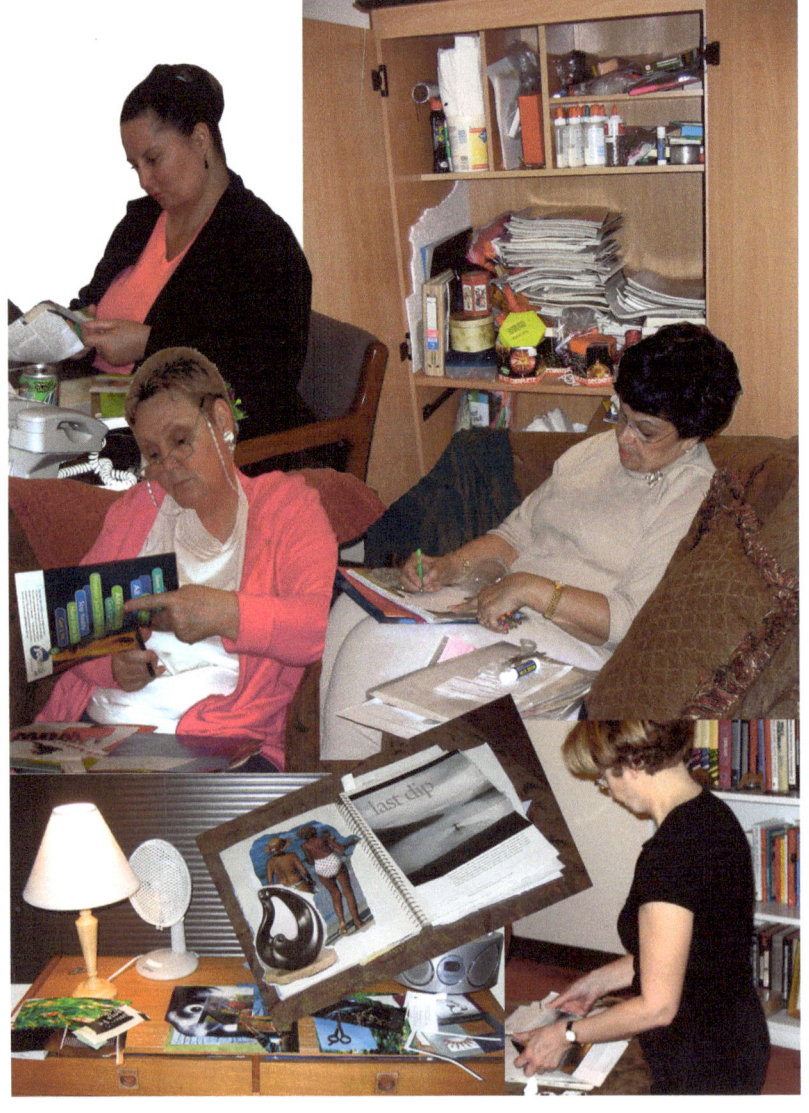

APPENDIX B

Additional Craft Supplies

- Magazines
- Fabric
- Wallpaper books
- Wood blocks
- Beads
- Pearls
- Glass jewels
- Sparkles and glitter
- String
- Colored feathers
- Sequins of many shapes
- Colored paper
- Colored foil
- Wool
- Ribbon
- Wire
- Confetti
- Wrapping paper
- Shredded paper
- Cotton balls
- Lace
- Acrylic paint
- Tempera paint
- Fabric Paint
- Colored and patterned tissue paper
- Bells
- Liquid laundry starch
- Tinsel
- Bottles of glue
- Glue guns

- Glue sticks
- Tacky glue
- Wire cutters
- Scissors
- Paint brushes
- Knives
- Construction paper
- Paper towel rolls
- Cardboard sheets
- Oatmeal boxes
- Styrofoam
- Roll of newsprint (end of roll from local news agency)
- Cardboard boxes
- Cardboard toilet tissue rolls
- Oil pastels
- Magic markers
- Bark
- Pastels
- Plastic and brown bags
- Glitter markers
- Raffia
- Dried leaves
- Dried fruit and flowers
- Silk or plastic flowers
- Driftwood
- Wood shavings
- Natural feathers
- Spanish moss
- Shells
- Sponges

- Twigs
- Plaster gauze
- Stickers
- Pine cones
- Gel pens
- Wood roses
- Stencils
- Homemade paper
- Decorative art papers by the Black Ink Company
- Stamps
- Stamp pads, and stamp rollers
- Embossing powder
- Edge accent scissors
- Templates and cutouts
- Calligraphy pens
- Toothpicks
- Masking tape
- Scotch tape
- Stapler and staples
- Milkweed
- Lichens
- Coral
- Dried sea weed
- Dried corn leaves and hair
- Polished stones
- Sea glass
- Colored clay (non-hardening and oven bake)
- Natural stones
- Polymer clay (Fimo, Sculpee)

www.ingramcontent.com/pod-product-compliance
Lightning Source LLC
Chambersburg PA
CBHW041457280526
45792CB00004B/1038